A
WORTHY
PIECE
of WORK

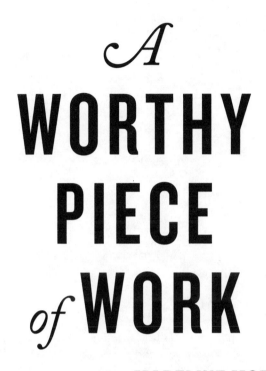

A WORTHY PIECE *of* WORK

THE UNTOLD STORY OF **MADELINE MORGAN** AND THE FIGHT FOR **BLACK HISTORY IN SCHOOLS**

MICHAEL HINES

Beacon Press | Boston

Beacon Press
Boston, Massachusetts
www.beacon.org

Beacon Press books
are published under the auspices of
the Unitarian Universalist Association of Congregations.

25 24 23 22   8 7 6 5 4 3 2 I

This book is printed on acid-free paper that meets the uncoated paper
ANSI/NISO specifications for permanence as revised in 1992.

Text design and composition by Kim Arney

"For Charlemae Rollins," by Gwendolyn Brooks. Reprinted By Consent of Brooks
Permissions. Credit for image on p. 26: Chicago Public Library, Madeline Stratton
Morris Papers, box 16, folder 4. Credit for image on p. 110: Chicago Public
Library, Madeline Stratton Morris Papers, box 16, folder 45.

Library of Congress Cataloguing in Publication Data is available for this title.
Library of Congress Control Number: 2022000437
Hardcover ISBN: 978-08070-0742-6
Ebook ISBN: 978-08070-0748-8

For Erica and Elijah

CONTENTS

INTRODUCTION

*N*OVEMBER 5, 1943—Pvt. Edward Butler, a Black soldier in the US Army, sent a letter back to the United States from North Africa. Written on the military's standard Victory Mail stationery, the letter was not to a sweetheart or family member, but to someone he had never met, an elementary school social studies teacher in Chicago, Illinois, half a world away. The letter read:

> Dear Mrs. Morgan,
>
> I just read an article about you and your work I writting [sic] to you to find out if I can get a copy of the Negroes History which was mention in Newsreel Magazine it is something I didn't learn in school. But would like to learn it now I'll be glad when we are called Brown Soldier instead of Negrosoldier We are fighting and working for the same cause as every one [else] from the States
> Your[s] Until,
> Edward[1]

Butler's wartime request seems strange at first, but he was not alone in finding Madeline Morgan (later Madeline Stratton Morris) and her "Negroes History" worthy of attention. Throughout the war years, hundreds of soldiers and civilians, principals and teachers, colleges and commissions, parents and students eagerly sought out Morgan and her pioneering work in Black history. By the spring of 1944, just a year after Butler's correspondence, Morgan shared that "hundreds of letters have been received expressing a desire to know something about the contributions of the Negro." The teacher's writing appeared in Black academic journals like the *Wilberforce Quarterly*, *Journal of Negro Education*, and *Negro History Bulletin*, as well as predominately white publications like the *Elementary English Review*, and even popular news magazines like *PM* and *Time*. The ideas and ideals of the primary schoolteacher from Chicago traveled "as far south as South America; as far north as Maine; as far west as California; as distant as Italy and Africa," and even to "the United States Office of Education in Washington D.C."[2]

The reason behind the widespread interest in Morgan's work from educators, scholars, and individuals like Pvt. Butler was that she had succeeded in spearheading one of the most profound educational efforts of the war years. Morgan had led a movement that resulted in the institution of Black history as part of the curriculum of Chicago's public schools, then the second largest school system in the nation. Her work, *The Supplementary Units for the Course of Instruction in Social Studies*, constituted an intellectual campaign against the foundations of American racial prejudice as bold and as necessary as the military effort to confront fascism abroad.

Hailed by Frayser Lane, civic director of Chicago's Urban League, as "one of the finest approaches to improvement in racial relations ever attempted," the units included the histories of West African civilizations and their connections to Black culture in the Americas and elsewhere, depictions of slavery that addressed the horrors of the Middle Passage and the plantation system, the stories of Black soldiers who defended democracy even while being denied its fruits, and the biographies of Black artists, politicians, activists, and social leaders from the country's founding to the present day.[3] The lessons combated the exclusion and marginalization of Black America found in white-authored textbooks and demanded a place for Black history at the center of the American story. As Morgan wrote in a note to teachers, "[The Negro] has contributed to every phase of American history. In adventure, science, education, art, music, war, and labor, he has played a part."[4]

Morgan's work served as a model for cities and school districts across the nation, and she advised politicians, religious and civic leaders, and educators interested in the promotion of racial tolerance throughout the mid-1940s. Despite her notoriety during the war years, however, she has received little scholarly attention in the almost century since. Compelling but incomplete glimpses of her appear in larger volumes on race and education, women's activism, and public history.[5] Yet a substantive work that explains her evolution as an educator, her success as a curriculum reformer and activist, and her legacy in the present has not yet been attempted. *A Worthy Piece of Work* addresses this absence, situating Morgan and her contributions within education during the 1930s and 1940s that garnered her national and international attention, within the broader movement for Black history and culture and the rise of pluralist and intercultural education during the Second World War.

The Early Black History Movement and the Alternative Black Curriculum

Morgan's efforts in the Chicago schools were part of a larger wave of scholarship and activism aimed at the preservation and promotion of Black history in the early twentieth century, an intellectual and social project that historian Pero Dagbovie terms the "early black history movement."[6] Although Black Americans' efforts to record and remember their past stretched back to the antebellum period, the years between 1915 and 1950 saw these early efforts expand, becoming highly organized and institutionalized. Carter G. Woodson, the Harvard-trained historian and educator remembered as the "Father of Negro History," both personified and precipitated this shift. In 1915, Woodson launched the Association for the Study of Negro Life and History, which, through its yearly conferences and its publications, the *Journal of Negro History* and the *Negro History Bulletin*, centralized and systematized the study of the Black past. At the same time, Negro History Week (the precursor to Black History Month), an annual campaign created under the auspices of the association, brought Black history into communities and classrooms, making the association's work broadly accessible.

Negro History Week, which Woodson described as "one of the most fortunate steps ever taken by the Association," revealed a major concern of the early Black history movement, the fight to reshape the school curriculum to which Black children were exposed.[7] White supremacy and anti-Black racism were deeply embedded in the curriculum of America's schools in the early twentieth century, particularly in history and social studies.[8] White-authored textbooks cast Africa as a primitive wilderness; omitted the histories of African civilizations before European colonization; justified American slavery as a benevolent and necessary (although regrettable) institution; painted the Civil War as a tragic struggle between equally noble causes; claimed Reconstruction to be a period of chaotic misrule by Black people and "carpetbaggers"; and portrayed Black Americans in the present as a social problem instead of a people. Taken together, these historical discourses sent a clear message that Black people were "racially inferior" and "deserved no equal place in American society."[9] The connection between the school curriculum and white supremacy, and the life-or-death consequences of that relationshiop, were clear to Woodson, who wrote that this struggle was of greater importance than even the fight against lynching because "there would be no lynching if it did not start in the schoolroom."[10]

Aware that America's schools distorted history in order to uphold the logic of white supremacy, Black historians, educators, and activists created their own textbooks, magazines, lesson plans, children's books, and other instructional materials. Scholar Alana Murray names these efforts the "alternative black curriculum," a powerful term I adopt here to refer broadly to the "pedagogical counter narrative" created by Black scholars in order to "provide a more accurate rendering of US and world history in the United States."[11] Woodson and the association were critical to the flowering of the alternative Black curriculum, and Woodson himself authored several groundbreaking textbooks including *The Negro in Our History* (1922), *The Story of the Negro Retold*

(1935), and *African Heroes and Heroines* (1939), each of which influenced generations of students and teachers.

In recent years, scholars have begun to shed light on both the early Black history movement and the alternative Black curriculum.[12] However, there is much more to uncover about how this movement took shape and the societal forces and individual personalities that propelled it. One under-studied aspect of this work has been the central role played by Black women. As Murray argues, the work of women like Nannie Helen Burroughs, Jessie Redmon Fauset, and Leila Amos Pendleton, though essential to shaping the alternative Black curriculum, has failed to garner the same attention as the scholarship of their male contemporaries and continues to be underappreciated.[13] Because of the intersectional weight of sexist and racist oppression, few Black women in the early twentieth century gained access to the kinds of credentials often associated with historical scholarship: PhDs and advanced coursework, faculty positions in universities and colleges, and publication in academic spaces. Yet, outside the bounds of the formal academy, Black women acted as "historians without portfolio" who were deeply involved in both history writing and history education as teachers, librarians, journalists, archivists, school founders, and administrators.[14] They organized themselves through teachers' associations, sororities, and women's clubs, sharing pedagogical knowledge and popularizing new materials and teaching methods across the country and beyond its borders. While the relative lack of status accorded to their roles meant that their stories were often overshadowed, it was these contributions, the "practical work of women," that brought the alternative Black curriculum and the larger Black history movement to life.[15]

A Worthy Piece of Work advances and critically expands our understanding of the history of Black women educators and their role in building the alternative Black curriculum in schools, taking Murray's original focus on the period from 1890 to 1940 and extending it into the pivotal years of the Second World War and beyond. Morgan's critique of the racism embedded in the official knowledge of America's schools exemplified the alternative Black curriculum, yet her race, gender, and position as a classroom teacher have led to a lack of scholarly engagement with her ideas. In the chapters that follow, I trace her development as an educator, the scope and content of her major curricular innovations, and the substantial gains as well as limitations and constraints she met with. To do so, I draw on the techniques of educational biography to make clear the "intersections between human agency and social structure" that defined Morgan's life and work.[16] Throughout, I consciously center Black women who have remained marginal in most works written on the early Black history movement. This includes not only Morgan but a constellation of other figures, such as librarians Vivian G. Harsh and Charlemae Rollins, principal Maudelle Bousfield, and teacher activist Onedia Cockrell, each of whose stories intersects with Morgan's own.

Intercultural Education and Interest Convergence

While the alternative Black curriculum and the early Black history movement took shape in the years between 1915 and 1950, Morgan's efforts came at a particular historical moment, the early 1940s, when events on the world's stage gave Black calls for equality and representation increased immediacy and resonance. The rise of European fascism in the 1930s, built on a foundation of virulent scientific racism, held a disturbing mirror to America's own deeply entrenched racial and religious prejudice, including anti-Black racism and antisemitism. As America's entry into the Second World War loomed on the horizon, the US sought to ideologically distance itself from its fascist enemies and unite Americans of various backgrounds behind the war effort. As part of this shift, the American press, civic organizations, religious groups, and importantly the public schools, began to embrace and emphasize racial and religious tolerance and intercultural understanding. As President Roosevelt declared, if the United States were to win the global conflict, it would take a "national unity that can know no limitations of race or creed or selfish politics."[17]

In schools, this new focus on interculturalism led to an explosion of programmatic and curricular experiments aimed at building tolerance and unity. From Detroit to New York, San Jose to Springfield, students read about the unique "cultural gifts" various ethnicities contributed to the American way of life, listened to radio programs that catalogued the accomplishments of Americans of divergent backgrounds, and watched films emphasizing brotherhood and cooperation.[18] The majority of intercultural education efforts were crafted by liberal white authors and aimed at expanding the idea of American citizenship to the children of minority groups from eastern and southern Europe. Black educators, however, also aligned themselves with interculturalism as a vehicle for voicing their own long-standing calls for respect and representation in the schools.

For Black teachers like Morgan, the war effort and the rise of intercultural education offered an opportunity to advance the goals of the early Black history movement. Throughout the war, Black educators made the case that the racism that pervaded American schools constituted not only an injustice against Black Americans but also an "imminent threat to American democracy," a glaring hole in the nation's defenses that could be exploited if left unchecked.[19] Morgan insisted that in order to bring the country together and deal with the rising racial tensions the war had brought to the fore, schools needed to deal squarely with the "injustices inflicted against Negro Americans," including the "mis-education" they were subjected to and the "popularly accepted racial superiority myth" that pervaded American education.[20]

Although scholars have recognized the shared features of intercultural education and the Black history movement, they have often seen the two as occurring in parallel with little or no intersection.[21] Educators like Morgan, however, drew from and contributed to both, complicating this assumption. She was active both in Black historical organizations like the Association for the Study of Negro Life and History and white-led intercultural ones like the National Council for the Social Studies, and as a result spoke to a broad interracial audience. *A Worthy Piece of Work* makes clear the connections that existed between the intercultural education movement and the Black history movement, especially at the level of individual teachers and schools.

In her bid to advance Black history in the schools, Morgan tied together the early Black history movement, interculturalism, and wartime solidarity. It was a strategy that bore fruit. In 1941, William H. Johnson, the white superintendent of Chicago's schools, endorsed Morgan's efforts, providing her with a platform and the resources of the city's Bureau of Curriculum. Johnson's move ensured that the resulting effort would be, as he put it, "an integral part of the curriculum, not alone for those schools whose membership is predominately Negro, but for all the public schools of Chicago."[22] The war brought Johnson and Morgan together in an instance of what scholar Derrick Bell described as "interest convergence," a moment where the self-interests of powerful whites and Black calls for justice intersect.[23] Morgan's goals were the promotion of Black equality and the reduction of white prejudice. Johnson's priority was to avoid interracial conflict as Chicago's schools and the broader society around them were engulfed in wartime debates about the meaning of citizenship, identity, and democracy. As he put the matter, "Self-preservation exacts a oneness in motive and in deed."[24] Both Johnson and Morgan came to embrace intercultural education and Black history as a means of achieving their ends, with powerful and unexpected results.

When the *Supplementary Units* were completed and formally made part of Chicago's curriculum on May 28, 1942, they stirred immediate recognition and national interest. Morgan became a familiar face in education journals, the popular press, and lecture halls, where crowds gathered to hear her explain her work. She advised school systems across the country and reached thousands of curious parents, teachers, administrators, civic and religious leaders, soldiers, and students. In the Black community, she was hailed for advancing the cause of Black history and laying an intellectual foundation on which Black demands for equality could stand. In the white community, she was sought out by intercultural educators who saw the need to better race relations, some from a desire for equity and equality, others because of the exigencies of war. This convergence of interests would be brief, however, fading in the postwar period as white authorities abandoned their advocacy for the curriculum Morgan had crafted. By 1950 her work would be largely forgotten.

This story of struggle, progress, and regression speaks to our contemporary moment in several ways. Today's educators and activists continue to grapple with an official curriculum that distorts and devalues Black history and culture. Given this reality, Morgan's story provides opportunities to think about current possibilities and potential pitfalls as "the act of reconstructing history is inextricably linked to . . . transforming the present and future."[25] Morgan's work shows the promise of curricular change initiated by teacher activists and arising from the needs of educators and the communities they represent. Her reliance on scholarly communities outside of the boundaries of the school system, including local history clubs, libraries, sororities, and civil rights groups, highlights the robust networks of support and sustenance that remain, although in different forms, in the present. Her adoption of wartime interculturalism speaks to the pragmatic ways in which Black educators have sought to elicit change in white-dominated school systems, and the national response she garnered points to the level of success she attained. At the same time, the disuse of her curriculum in the postwar period calls into question whether and how Black history might more deeply penetrate the US curriculum, and how shifts in education originating in moments of crisis might more successfully solidify into lasting change.

Organization of Chapters

A Worthy Piece of Work is divided into six chapters. Chapter 1 traces Morgan's development as an educator and activist from her birth in 1906 until 1940, the year she set in motion her plan to bring Black history to Chicago's schools. Throughout the chapter, I argue that Morgan's unique perspective and pedagogy grew, first and foremost, from the intellectual milieu of Chicago's Black South Side and its array of interconnected associations, social clubs, civic groups, sororities, and civil rights organizations. Key sites of support and sustenance for Morgan included the sorority Phi Delta Kappa, the Association for the Study of Negro Life and History, and the George Cleveland Hall public library. In addition, Morgan's formal education took her outside the Black community to majority-white institutions such as Englewood High School, the Chicago Normal College, and Northwestern University. Her time in these spaces familiarized her with progressive educational techniques and philosophies, but it also introduced her to the distance between the rhetoric espoused by many white progressives and the racism they ignored or endorsed in practice. Both white and Black spaces shaped her distinct outlook on race and education, and led her to see schools as a powerful mechanism for social change.

Chapter 2 deals with Morgan's development of the *Supplementary Units* between 1940 and 1942, placing her efforts within the larger context of the Second World War, Black responses, and the intercultural education movement. Inspired by Chicago's American Negro Exposition of 1940, Morgan and other Black educators launched a campaign to make Black history visible within the curriculum of Chicago's public schools. This effort was informed by the larger spirit of activism developing within the Black community in response to the Second World War, which included protests against the racial segregation of the military and discrimination in civilian defense work. One response to this climate of dissent was the rise of a movement for intercultural education, backed by liberal religious organizations, civic associations, and civil rights groups. Making its way into education, where it was embraced by white educators and their Black peers, though far more critically by the latter, intercultural education formed an essential backdrop against which Morgan's efforts took place. As the war brought the interests of Black teachers and white officials in Chicago's public schools into alignment, an example of Derrick Bell's theory of interest convergence, Morgan was able to use the historical moment to secure a platform she might otherwise have been denied.

Chapter 3 offers the first complete analysis of the product of Morgan's efforts, the *Supplementary Units for the Course of Instruction in the Social Studies*, written by Morgan and her research assistant, Bessie M. King. Using Alana Murray's alternative Black curriculum as a framework, I argue that Morgan's materials were purposefully crafted to rebuff the racism embedded in the white-authored curricula of her time and to put forward an alternative vision of Black history and humanity, placing her alongside a long line of scholars acting in this tradition. The chapter concentrates on several aspects of Morgan's curriculum, including her reconceptualization of Africa and its civilizations; her revisionist account of slavery, the Civil War, and Reconstruction; her connection of African communities to the greater diaspora; her attention to Black military contributions; and her coverage of local Black history within the city of Chicago.

Chapter 4 explores the reception of the *Supplementary Units* both locally in Chicago and nationally, between 1942 and 1945. Morgan's efforts were quickly recognized as unique and important within the Black community, where she was lauded by other educators interested in making Black history a part their own local curricula. In the white community, Morgan's work was also heralded, but with an emphasis on its potential use as a tool to build white students' interracial understanding and to temper Black resentment over racial injustice. It was a mission that seemed even more critical in the aftermath of the riots of 1943, which saw white mobs viciously assault Black and Brown communities across the US in attempts to slow the social and economic gains made by minorities during the war years. Both the *Supplementary Units* and the figure behind them seemed to offer a measured and moderate response to the tensions boiling over across the nation. As a result of both Black and white responses to her work, Morgan found herself at the center of national discussions of race, history, and representation throughout this period. Morgan was called on as a speaker, published in academic journals, was interviewed by *Time* magazine and other popular outlets, advised intercultural education projects in several cities, and sent hundreds of copies of her work to other educators.

Chapter 5 explores how the *Supplementary Units* were implemented at the classroom level. While educational policies are written and adopted at the levels of cities, districts, and states, their enactment happens at the more intimate level of the classroom, where individual teachers and students navigate new curricula and objectives. Through a critical analysis of responses written by Morgan's Black students at Emerson Elementary and an account written by teacher Grace Markwell, who was working with white students in the suburb of Brookfield, Illinois, I find that the *Supplementary Units* opened up new space within both white and Black classrooms for discussions of race and history, and ultimately social justice and equality. While it is impossible to gauge how a particular lesson or experience ultimately shaped the attitudes or beliefs of individual students, opportunites to facilitate such changes were important in and of themselves. At the same time, this potential could go only so far in a context of schools and neighborhoods that remained largely segregated.

Chapter 6 follows Morgan and her work into the postwar period, from 1945 to 1950. While the war had brought the interests of Black educators and white policy makers into alignment, this moment was brief. In the aftermath of the conflict, new battle lines were drawn on the home front as Black Chicagoans fought to hold and expand the gains of the war years while whites fought to reassert control and dominance. Morgan's curriculum fell from use in the changed climate of the late 1940s, years marked by postwar housing shortages, increasing educational and geographic segregation, and escalating racial violence. However, Morgan and other committed educators like her continued to fight for decades to come, setting the stage for struggles that continue unabated into the present.

A
WORTHY
PIECE
of WORK

CHAPTER 1

"KNOWLEDGE IS POWER ONLY IF IT IS PUT INTO ACTION"

The Making of Madeline Morgan

*J*ANUARY 10, 1944—Ora MacDonald, editor of the *Northwestern University Alumni News*, needed to be sure. She was looking for information on a recent alumna of the education program. Apparently, the teacher had caused a sensation "all over the nation" by authoring "three booklets on Negro history now used in 353 elementary schools" in Chicago alone. MacDonald, perhaps a bit embarrassed to have read all this in the Associated Press clippings instead of finding out earlier, was now keen to see if Madeline R. Morgan, Northwestern BS '36 and MA '41, was the same woman behind the "Negro history" effort. "If you *are* [emphasis original] the teacher referred to," MacDonald insisted, "please send us some biographical information about yourself."[1]

Three days later, Morgan responded to MacDonald's queries. After confirming that she was in fact "the *Madeline R. Morgan* [emphasis original] referred to," she went on to give a short biographical sketch, including her educational background and the clubs and associations in which she took part.[2] What Morgan chose to highlight revealed a great deal about her background, vision, and values. The letter described her participation in the tightly connected web of Black women's clubs, sororities, civil rights groups, and academic and scholarly societies that supported and sustained Black women's activism in early twentieth-century Chicago. In addition, her outlook was also informed by her experiences in largely white educational institutions, including Englewood High School, Chicago Normal College, and Northwestern University. These interconnected strands came together to shape Morgan's unique pedagogy and politics.

Morgan's early life, education, and organizational experiences equipped her with the skills and dispositions to take up the project of introducing Black history into the Chicago Public Schools at a time when Black voices were systematically excluded from the curriculum. Her approach was nurtured by the explosion of Black communal and institutional life that evolved in Chicago as a result of the Great Migration, rooted in the activist traditions of Black women educators, and molded by her experiences, both positive and negative, in the city's predominantly white educational spaces. Drawing on this background, Morgan became a teacher activist dedicated to the use of education as a lever to elicit broad social change. This outlook would inspire her mission to promote Black history and incorporate it into the school curriculum.

"The Nucleus of Another Society": Growing Up in the Great Migration
Madeline Morgan was born Madeline Robinson in Chicago on August 14, 1906, to Estella Mae and John Henry Robinson. She was the eldest child of a family that would eventually include six children: four more daughters, Vivian, Eydth, Zana, and Adrionno, along with a son, Robert. Estella Mae was originally from Chicago, and John Henry had made his way north from Ronceverte, West Virginia, and spent time in Philadelphia before settling in the Midwest. When he arrived in Chicago in 1903, John gained work as an elevator operator in the maintenance department of Butler Brothers, which along with Sears, Roebuck and Company and Montgomery Ward, was a major retailer with national reach through its independent chain stores and

shopping catalogue services. Robinson kept the position with Butler Brothers for forty-five years, creating a foundation of stability his family would use to realize opportunities that had been unattainable for previous generations.

When he moved north to Chicago, Robinson became part of a steady stream of southern Black migrants that would swell to a flood in the decades to come. Between 1910 and 1920, the city's Black population increased by an astonishing 148.5 percent, growing from 44,103 to 109,594. In the next decade, it doubled again, reaching 233,903 by 1930.[3] This demographic shift was part of the larger Great Migration, a movement that saw millions of Black Americans abandon the Jim Crow South, a region the *Chicago Defender* described as a land of "blight, murdered kin," and "strangled ambitions."[4] Migrants traveled north and west to cities like Detroit, Philadelphia, Oakland, Chicago, and New York, in pursuit of social equality and economic opportunity. Although they often found life in these urban centers far from perfect, migrants felt that their journeys enabled them to take firmer hold of the "prerequisites of American citizenship," including access to better jobs, housing, and schools.[5]

The Great Migration transformed the northern and western cities that acted as its major harbors. In Chicago, the South Side, which had been occupied by a small but stalwart Black community since the nineteenth century, expanded into Bronzeville, a city within a city, boasting its own vibrant and largely autonomous Black cultural, intellectual, and political spaces. As one early observer commented about Black Chicagoans, "They make their own wit. Their own music from their own views. And they live their own lives. They do not constitute the fringe of white society. They are the nucleus of another society, and one in which true and great enjoyment is to be had."[6] The financial independence of the Binga State Bank and Liberty Life Insurance Company, the commercial empires of the Overton Hygienic Company and Poro Beauty College, the rise of the Black press through the *Chicago Bee, Chicago Whip,* and nationally prominent *Chicago Defender,* the political influence exerted by pioneering congressman

Oscar De Priest, the blossoming cultural creativity expressed through Archibald Motley's brush and Mahalia Jackson's voice—each of these pointed to a community finding a new measure of strength, solidarity, and self-determination in the urban North. By the 1930s and 1940s this growth would lead to the flowering of artistic and cultural production known as the "Chicago Black Renaissance," placing the city in competition with New York's Harlem as the center of Black American life.[7]

Black migrants came to Chicago hopeful that they would be able to build spaces where they could live with more freedom and autonomy than they had in the regions they left behind. However, new opportunities existed alongside familiar challenges. As the Black community expanded, white Chicagoans, who "without the threat of a significant black population" had largely ignored the Black presence within the city, began to view it as a potential threat.[8] As the migration continued, white fears of a "Negro invasion" led policy makers to use political and legal measures to limit the expansion of Black neighborhoods and confine new arrivals to increasingly under-resourced and overcrowded stretches of the South Side.[9] Black families who attempted to escape these conditions by moving to other areas of the city met with legal resistance from white neighborhood associations, who used restrictive covenants to prohibit property owners from selling or renting to Black buyers, and street-level violence, including physical assaults, arson, and the firebombing of homes and businesses. Between July 1, 1917 and March 1, 1921, alone, fifty-eight separate incidents, an average of "one race bombing every twenty days," were recorded in Chicago.[10]

The horrific extent of white racial terrorism became clear during the so-called Red Summer of 1919, as violence flared across the country in the aftermath of the First World War and the return of Black and white soldiers. White mobs, fearful of economic competition, Black migration, and increasing postwar demands for racial equality, attacked Black communities in both the rural South and the urban North. In Chicago, where white violence toward the growth and visibility of the Black population had already set the city on edge, riots broke out on July 27. The inciting incident was the death of a Black child only four years older than Madeline, seventeen-year-old Eugene Williams, who was attacked for swimming in an area of the lake-shore claimed by whites. The ensuing confrontation between Black and white witnesses, the failure of police to arrest those responsible, and the rumors that spread like wildfire through the city afterward began a spiral of violence and reprisal. White mobs gathered and invaded Black neighborhoods, pulled Black passengers from public transportation, and assaulted Black men, women, and children in the streets. Madeline endured the "nights of terror" as gunshots pierced the peace of her childhood, and her father stood guard in the window of their flat on Dearborn Street, working with neighbors to protect their property from the mobs that tore through the South Side.[11] By the time federal troops restored order seven days later, 38 were dead, 537 injured, and over 1,000 left homeless.[12] The riots offered stark proof that the "color line," W. E. B. Du Bois's phrase for the rigidly maintained societal divide that kept Black and white America separate and unequal, remained a defining feature of Black life in the North as well as the South.[13]

"Constant Friction": Black Education in the Migration Era

The 1919 riot showed Black migrants to Chicago that their access to equal jobs, housing, and social services would be bitterly contested. This reality was also reflected in the city's school system. For many migrants, the opportunity to secure a better education for themselves and their children figured prominently into the choice to come north.[14] John Henry Robinson counted it among his greatest blessings that, despite his limited formal education, five of his six children were able to attend college, a testament to the increased access to education he was able to secure for them in his new home. Chicago offered longer school terms, better trained teachers and administrators, and more re-sources than Black families could access in the rural South. Critically,

Chicago's schools were also free of the legally mandated segregation of school facilities found throughout the Jim Crow south.[15]

Despite legal equality, however, white policy makers during the 1920s and 1930s increasingly employed legal and bureaucratic strategies to erect systems of racial separation. As historian Worth Kamili Hayes points out, white officials in Chicago soon became "adept at making local schools both separate and unequal."[16] They manipulated the boundaries of attendance zones in ways that divided school catchment areas along racial lines. They used the system of branch schools, through which multiple buildings could be combined under shared administrative control, to create separate Black and white schools that shared little beyond a name in common. When these methods failed, permissive transfers, which were given at the discretion of the board of education with little or no accountability, provided an additional mechanism for white families to flee demographically changing schools.

As these strategies of segregation took hold, Black students were isolated in schools that were older, more overcrowded, and less resourced than majority-white schools. When the Chicago Commission on Race Relations surveyed the twenty-two schools with the highest populations of Black students in the early 1920s, they found that eighteen lacked lunchroom facilities, fifteen had no bathroom, and nineteen had no designated gymnasium. Only five of the schools had been built after the year 1900. In comparison, over half of the majority-white schools studied were housed in buildings constructed after the turn of the century. Black students at Moseley Elementary, the oldest in the district, were taught in a dilapidated structure built in 1856, five years before the start of the Civil War.[17] These conditions had dire consequences for students' learning, physical safety, and health. In 1936, some seventy students at Hayes Elementary, built in 1867, contracted trench mouth, a severe gum infection caused by the buildup of bacteria in the mouth, which leads to bleeding ulcerations. In 1938, the south wing of Colman Elementary, which had been built in 1887 and was badly in need of repair, burned to the ground, leaving 1,560 pupils without adequate space to attend classes. Parents had protested these conditions long before, petitioning the board of education to repair the building, but their voices had gone unacknowledged.[18]

Racial segregation and inequality would play a direct role in Morgan's early educational experiences. The household initially lived at 3736 Dearborn Street but moved south to 5440 Dearborn in the Washington Park neighborhood, and Madeline attended nearby Farren Elementary School. Like other majority Black schools in the city, Farren was housed in one of the district's oldest buildings, constructed in 1898.[19] Despite the school's majority Black student population, Madeline remembered that her teachers—Ms. Stein, Mrs. Eberstein, Ms. Mason, and Ms. Lady—were almost all "Irish or Jewish" in background. This reality reflected another aspect of northern educational inequality, the discrimination in hiring and placement faced by Black teachers. Would-be Black educators were routinely denied credentials through subjective licensure exams given by white administrators, left to languish in the ranks of long-term substitutes instead of receiving permanent positions, or relegated to a handful of posts in majority Black schools where, even there, they constituted a minority of the faculty. Morgan witnessed only one Black teacher in her time at Farren, the proper and petite Ms. Patton. Even though she never had Patton as a teacher, Morgan identified with her and felt it was significant to have "one of us in that school." When Morgan herself became a teacher decades later, her first assignment would place her in a school with a majority of Black students taught by an almost entirely white staff, a pattern that would continue for decades to come.[20]

Despite the age of the building and the lack of Black faculty, Morgan's time at Farren was relatively positive. She enjoyed academics immensely, especially reading, and her early aptitude earned her attention and praise from her instructors. Studious and earnest, Morgan often completed the work for both her grade level and the level above, which led her principal to promote her to more advanced courses. Outside of the school day, Morgan found other ways to continue her learning. As she recalled later, "I was always teaching in Sunday school or some little club, or something like that. I was always involved in something, whether I was involved as a teacher, or helper." These early experiences proved to be dress rehearsals for her future life's work.[21]

Morgan remembered little outright discrimination at Farren. This would change abruptly when she reached Englewood High School. Located at Sixty-Second Street and Stuart Avenue, the school, south of the Robinsons' home, sat in a predominantly white neighborhood, not the more ethnically diverse enclave that surrounded Farren, and Black youth were only a small fraction of the student body. The school and community were far less welcoming, and for the first time Madeline was made "aware that she was different."[22] Englewood's Black students endured frequent indignities. They were forced to enter through a separate door at the back of the school, ignored by many of their teachers, and routinely given failing grades regardless of the quality of their work. Morgan's experience in one class in particular, French, made this bigotry painfully clear. No matter her effort, she received failing grades, but when she was assigned to another teacher she noticed a dramatic shift: "a woman who was here, [an] exchange teacher from France . . . who did not know about segregation and discrimination, and I was put into her class, and then I began to get an S, superior, and I couldn't understand what had happened that I would get a superior, and I had been getting D['s] all the time, you know, but that's what happened."[23]

If Black students at Englewood faced racism in their formal instruction, informal interactions could be just as fraught. Although they were able to participate in school activities like orchestra, literary societies, and athletic teams, the interactions between Black and white students had clearly defined limits. For instance, a dean at Englewood interviewed as part of a report by the Chicago Commission on Race Relations in 1922 recalled that at social events and school dances, "five or six colored children" would always attend and were "welcomed by the whites." While they laughed and joked with their white classmates in between songs, however, the black students "always danced together," a clear sign of the social prescriptions that silently suffused every interaction. Any exchange that brought white and Black students into close social contact, especially of a nature that could be potentially sexual, was wholly unacceptable.[24]

The experience of Ellis Reid, one of Morgan's classmates, served as a stark reminder of the razor's edge that Black students walked in hostile white school settings. Reid was, by every account, an excellent student and an active participant in school life. A member of the school's reserve officer training corps, or ROTC, he was on the verge of being promoted to the rank of major. On December 5, 1923, he was placed as a guard for a performance of a school play, instructed by his superior officer not to allow anyone to pass through his assigned entrance once the program began. When a white girl approached him during the middle of the performance and asked to be let in, Reid refused her entry as he had been instructed. The girl then attempted to walk past him, but Reid blocked the door with his arm, forming a physical barrier. In return for the unpardonable breach of "insulting a white girl," Reid was attacked by six white students and barely managed to escape by hiding in a cloakroom and exiting through another door. The matter only worsened when the school's administration became involved. Instead of protecting Reid, Principal James E. Armstrong gave tacit approval to the actions of Reid's attackers by sending him home for an indefinite period without the benefit of an investigation. In order to appease white students and parents, Armstrong ultimately dismissed Reid from the school entirely. While he admitted that Reid was "a fine boy" and "faithful student" caught in a situation "for which he is not entirely to blame," the administrator justified the dismissal as a move made to save the school from the possibility of a race riot. The message to students like Madeline was clear: Black youth could not expect fair treatment in Chicago's schools, regardless of their intelligence, position, or talent, especially if they attempted to act as equals with their white peers.[25]

"A Cotton Picker in the South and . . . a Forgotten People in the North":
Black History and Identity in the Schools

Black students at Englewood had to contend not only with the racism embedded in the school's daily routines and formal and informal interactions; they also found it in the curriculum they were made to learn. A *Chicago Defender* article from 1928, three years after Morgan graduated, showed the extent to which prejudice was still part of the standard course of instruction. The article took issue with the textbook *History of the United States*, written by white minister and educator Henry William Elson, whom the paper noted "seems to have taken an unusual delight in spreading the kind of propaganda generally accepted throughout the South." In his text, Elson told his young readers that African Americans were biologically inferior, a "listless, aimless class who aspire to nothing: who are content to live in squalor and ignorance"; that Reconstruction after the Civil War had been little more than a failed experiment in Negro rule and "unnatural relations" between the races; and that the future progress of the country depended on racial separation and the subservience of Black citizens to the benevolent paternalism of white leadership as "the negro is quite safe and his happiness secured under the white man's government." Enraged that such egregious sentiments could be endorsed by the Chicago schools, the *Defender* fumed that Elson's text deserved to be committed to "the doubtful honor of a lakeside bonfire."[26]

While Elson's work was certainly appalling, its racist claims fell well within the mainstream of US history texts at the time. The vast majority of early twentieth-century history texts reflected similar assumptions, and other textbooks approved for use by Chicago's school board, including *The Story of Our Country* by Ruth and Willis Mason West, *Exploring American History* by Mabel Casner and Ralph Henry Gabriel, and *America's Roots in the Past* by Daniel Beeby, himself a principal at Chicago's Oglesby School, showed the same disregard for and dehumanization of Black Americans that characterized Elson's work. Social studies and history texts reflected and reinforced the anti-Black racism that infected every aspect of American daily life and material culture in the early twentieth century, from nursery rhymes and dime-store novels to advertisements, newspapers, radio programs, magazines, and films. These popular manifestations of racist thought were legitimated by the official knowledge produced by white philosophers, anthropologists, historians, and schoolteachers, who gave "scientific justification" for the unequal status of Black people and "helped to bolster firmly held beliefs that racial hierarchies were an outcome of a natural unfolding of human capacity."[27] Through school curricula, white academics and educators strengthened the structural logic of white supremacy while granting it the facade of objectivity, detachment, and rationality.

For Black students, whether in racially mixed schools or increasingly segregated in all-Black settings, the memory of these distorted histories lingered long into adulthood. As Morgan would later recall: "During my elementary and high school years our textbooks only portrayed the Afro-American as a cotton picker in the South and we were a forgotten people in the North. . . . We were portrayed as savages with no cultural background or as docile people who were happy and enjoyed singing and dancing to the tune of the banjo."[28] Even in her youth, she agreed with the *Chicago Defender's* assertion that texts like Elson's needed to be "ironed out" and replaced with accurate and truthful histories. Her eventual career as a teacher would give Morgan the ideological tools and the opportunity to do just that.[29]

"I Immediately Knew I Wanted to Go": Pedagogy and Progressivism at Chicago Normal College and Northwestern University

Morgan's early education had exposed her to both the promise of education and the reach of racial bigotry. After graduating from Englewood High School, she chose to apply to Chicago Normal College, following the three-year elementary teacher-training course between 1926 and 1929. She had always been drawn to teaching, leading small lessons at youth clubs and Sunday schools to which she belonged. After high school, however, Morgan was encouraged by those around her to pursue education more seriously. As she put it, "I immediately knew I wanted to go . . . that's all I heard about . . . so I went to [Chicago] Teachers College right away."[30]

The advice Morgan received to pursue a career in the classroom was not unusual for Black women of her era. For those who had the means to support further education and training, teaching held one of the few options for white-collar employment open to Black women and promised a measure of economic autonomy and social status not found elsewhere. Beyond personal and professional satisfaction, teaching also offered an avenue to contribute to the progress of the race. Since the antebellum period, Black education had been inextricably tied to political and social progress and the battle against white supremacy and oppression.[31] As teachers, Black women transformed schoolhouses into critical sites for social activism, implementing practices that "imbued the tenets found in critical pedagogy, social justice, and liberatory consciousness."[32] In Chicago, as in other cities, they acted as "activists, organizers, educators, and intellectuals, who theorized and implemented efforts to improve education for Black children."[33]

As scholar Paula Giddings has asserted, being an educator "at once made them [Black women] part of this racial uplift movement, gave them status, offered an opportunity to work in one of the few professions open to them, and gave them the means to overcome some of the restrictive attitudes toward the middle-class woman's role as silent and subservient homemaker."[34] Morgan's early experiences with racism and education at Farren and Englewood had begun to awaken this sense of mission within her. Her time training for the classroom at Chicago Normal College would make the need for such work even more clear.

Originally founded in 1867 as the Cook County Normal School, Chicago Normal College had earned a national reputation in the half century before Morgan began her time there. Vaunted educators such as Francis Parker and Ella Flagg Young had served as directors in previous years, bringing "international prestige," and the school was a bastion of the experimentalist approach that became known as progressive education by the early twentieth century.[35] Progressive education, much like the larger progressive movement, was dynamic and multifaceted, containing competing and oftentimes contradictory impulses. Peda-gogically, however, the educators, social workers, theorists, and philoso-phers who made up this wide-ranging movement were held together by a desire to bridge the divide between schools and the broader society, and to make students active participants in reimagining and changing the world around them.[36] While earlier generations of teachers focused on instilling orderliness, obedience, and deference in their students, of-ten through strict standards of behavior and rote memorization and routine, progressive educators attempted to help students develop their own ways of seeing and engaging with the world through the interpre-tation of experiences both in and outside of the classroom.

Chicago Normal College trained its teachers to embrace broad notions of democratic citizenship within their classrooms and tie academic pursuits to these wider progressive social goals. The De-partment of History and Civics, for instance, stressed that its courses would prepare teacher candidates to "cultivate a scientific mind to-wards social institutions and social problems."[37] Overall, the college stressed "open mindedness," a "progressive spirit," and "a will to be a factor in constructive social activities" as laudable goals for both teach-ers and students.[38] This "progressive spirit," however, did not make the college a more hospitable place for its few Black students. Morgan was one of only a handful of Black teacher candidates to attend the college during the 1920s, and she faced similar social barriers to her high school days, though that isolation may have been mitigated by events outside the school as she married Thomas Morgan in 1926. She made the most of opportunities for involvement, participating in the Women's Athletic Association, which sponsored basketball, tennis, and other teams and the Fellowship Club, which organized social ac-tivities on campus. Yet the inconsistency between the stated ideals of white progressive institutions and their treatment of Black people in practice left Morgan cold.

As she trained for the classroom, Morgan was exposed to the lim-ited reach of progressive education with regard to race and racism. One incident during her time as a teacher in training made this particularly clear: "Sharply I was awakened as a student in a history class, at Chicago Normal College, when the history instructor said that he had never read nor heard of a contribution or an achievement by a Negro. There I was, the only black in the division and could not defend nor answer about my background. I had not been taught."[39] Incensed by her instructor's assertion that Black people had played no part in the history of the world, paralyzed and embarrassed by her own lack of knowledge, Morgan found a new direction for the progressive pedagogy she was learning: "As I sat there I vowed that when I became a teacher—no student would ever leave my classroom without some knowledge of the history of Afro-Americans." As she began to teach, Morgan would take the pedagogies and approaches of progressive education but apply them to realities that her white contemporaries rarely addressed.

After Chicago Normal College, Morgan continued to pursue education, this time at Northwestern University. She enrolled in courses at its newly established McKinlock campus, located in downtown Chicago, which directly appealed to working students by bringing together numerous training and professional programs such as law, business, and education. Morgan took courses at Northwestern beginning in 1933 and received a BS from the institution in 1936 and an MA in 1941, both in education.

If her time at Chicago Normal College had begun to build her character as an educator, Morgan's years at Northwestern completed this process. Her arrival in the early 1930s coincided with the appointment of a new dean, Ernest O. Melby, a theorist and writer who was prominent in the Progressive Education Association (PEA) and who served on the board of directors of the nation's leading progressive journal, the *Social Frontier*. Melby's "primary objective" during his tenure was "to make Northwestern the model progressive teacher training institution in the nation."[40] To this end, the School of Education began to incorporate the latest social sciences, including "psychology, sociology, political science and economics"; classes were reorganized to concentrate on the practical problems of classrooms and communities; and students were encouraged to participate more democratically in their own education through increased choice in their courses of study. These changes reflected Melby's deep belief that the school could and should act as "the primary vehicle for reforming society" and that teachers should leave Northwestern prepared to work for change alongside their students.[41] As he stated in an annual report in 1939–40, Melby aimed for "an education which has effective social action as its goal."[42]

Chicago Normal College and Northwestern University strengthened several of the values Morgan would carry throughout her life: a concern with the connection between schools and communities; the importance of education in fostering democratic participation in society; the need to adapt the curriculum to address the real-world needs of students; and the responsibility of educators to address social ills. However, the change Morgan sought would be dictated as much by the failings of these educational institutions as by their successes. While the progressive movement encouraged examination of several aspects of American economic and social life, discussions of race, in particular the disenfranchisement and oppression of African Americans, never constituted more than a marginal concern for most white progressive educators. Worse still, measures endorsed by many white progressives, from IQ tests to student tracking, actively reinforced existing racial prejudice, delimiting the very goals of democracy and equality they espoused.[43] Black educators, on the other hand, knew that racial justice must be central to any substantive democratic pedagogical vision, and they adapted progressive education toward their own liberatory ends. Morgan's determination to see Black history incorporated into the Chicago schools was a combination of the tradition of uplift and activism of Black educators and the education for social action preached by her progressive contemporaries.

"A for Anderson—B for Bethune": Teaching Black History and Finding Community in Chicago's Schools

Morgan's time at Northwestern coincided with the first years of her teaching career. In 1933 she received her first school assignment, a position teaching sixth grade English and social studies at Chicago's Emerson Elementary. Located at 1700 West Walnut Street, on the city's West Side, the school was in a racially changing section of the city, as the small Black population grew and whites abandoned the area in turn. As was the case for most Black schools, Emerson was housed in an aging building, one that dated to 1884 and lacked gymnasium and auditorium spaces, forcing the faculty to block off the surrounding streets for recess periods and use the cramped basement for physical education. The school community also suffered from the ravages of the Great Depression, which disproportionally impacted Black Chicagoans already on the bottom of the social ladder. Despite these challenges, however, Morgan was enthusiastic about her new undertaking and determined to make it successful.[44]

As she began teaching, Morgan made it her mission to weave Black history into her curriculum. To achieve this goal, she found and drew on fresh networks of support and sustenance. These included the Association for the Study of Negro Life and History, the George Cleveland Hall Branch of the Chicago Public Library, and the National Sorority of Phi Delta Kappa.

THE ASSOCIATION FOR THE STUDY OF NEGRO LIFE AND HISTORY
The first and largest source of support for Morgan as she sought to make Black history a greater part of her work was the Association for the Study of Negro Life and History, or ASNLH. Founded in Chicago in 1915, the ASNLH was the creation of Carter G. Woodson, the scholar and educator who more than any other figure defined and championed the Black history movement of the early twentieth century. Woodson was deeply critical of mainstream American education, which he argued taught the Black child "that he has no worthwhile past, that his race has done nothing significant since the beginning of time, and that there is no evidence that he will ever achieve anything great."[45] In order to counter the dehumanization and devaluing of Black life, Woodson focused on the production and dissemination of new counterhegemonic knowledge concerning the Black experience. Through

countless reports, studies, journal articles, speeches, conferences, and textbooks, Woodson laid out his intellectual framework. The ASNLH adopted Woodson's blueprint, which was then elaborated on by Black educators throughout the country.

Acting out the mission of the association in the schools were thousands of Black teachers, the majority of them women, who made up the organization's rank and file. As historian Pero Dagbovie relates, these women "set up activities in schools, such as book displays and pageants; they worked hard to advertise Negro History Week celebrations; and they established branches, clubs, and study groups throughout the country."[46] A telling sign of the centrality of classroom teachers within the ASNLH was the creation of the *Negro History Bulletin* in 1937. Less academic in focus than the association's flagship publication, the *Journal of Negro History*, the bulletin was specifically geared toward teachers and their work, and included biographical articles on prominent Black figures, school news reports from around the nation, and reviews of Black history books written for classroom use. As an ASNLH pamphlet stated, "While this periodical is sponsored by the Association for the Study of Negro Life and History, it is an organ of the schools—something for the children. It has resulted from needs which have been disclosed among those who are trying to base the education of the Negro upon the Negro himself."[47] Teachers set the tone and direction of the periodical, formed a majority of the editorial staff, and contributed articles and student work, making the bulletin "an arena in which black women, mainly schoolteachers and social activists, could articulate their concerns about educating black youth, reforming American society, and uplifting the masses of their people."[48] In the years ahead, the *Bulletin* would prove a pivotal space for Morgan's own curriculum theorizing.

Joining the ASNLH in the early 1930s meant that Morgan became part of what historian Jarvis Givens has called an "insurgent intellectual network," a vigorous intellectual community that was both national and local.[49] In Chicago, members organized Black history clubs at their schools and created lessons for classroom use. At

Douglas Elementary, for example, teachers Mavis B. Mixon, Julma B. Crawford, Mary Williamson, and Charlotte Stratton were involved in coordinating a Negro History Club that met throughout the year. The association's *Negro History Bulletin* also proved popular with Chicago's Black educators, with 50 percent of teachers at Douglas, 75 percent of teachers at Forrestville, and 100 percent of the teachers at Keith subscribing to the publication in 1942, according to the *Chicago Defender*.[50] Morgan's involvement in the association would give her intellectual resources, a platform to share her work with others, and eventually the support of Woodson himself as she began to consider her own plans to produce and disseminate Black history.

In addition to subscribing to the *Bulletin* and fostering Negro History Clubs at their schools, Chicago's Black teachers embraced the celebration of Negro History Week with passion, creating special displays that were open to view by community members. Morgan's students wrote biographies of Black leaders, put together encyclopedias of notable African Americans, and clipped newspaper articles on Black achievement to share with the class. Morgan would later recall, "In order to teach about Black leaders I initiated a class project which was to be ready in February. Our class project was to make an A.B.C. notebook. A for [Marian] Anderson—B for [Mary McLeod] Bethune, C for [George Washington] Carver etc. Newspaper magazine pictures and articles were required. The project began to involve parents who helped their children, and the parents began to buy more magazines and newspapers."[51] This project, in which Morgan's dedication to furthering the knowledge of Black history was enacted through teaching that involved not just the students but the broader community as well, was a synthesis of her training and her own experiences.

THE GEORGE CLEVELAND HALL LIBRARY   While association meetings and school classrooms marked major sites for Morgan to draw from in her work reshaping the narratives surrounding Black history, another critical space was provided by the George Cleveland Hall Branch of the Chicago Public Library. Opened in January 1932, the branch was named after Hall, a physician at Chicago's Provident Hospital and a prominent member of Chicago's African American elite, who was the first African American to hold a seat on Chicago's library board. It was Hall's efforts that convinced his friend, Julius Rosenwald, the Sears and Roebuck executive and philanthropist whose foundation donated millions to Black educational causes, to put up the initial financing for a library catering to Chicago's growing Black community. While Hall himself died the year prior to the library's completion, the impressive building with its stone facade and Italian Renaissance design was named in his honor and became a resource for generations of Black scholars, writers, professionals, and activists. Serving a population of 250,000 to 300,000 residents, the Hall Branch was the intellectual center of the Black Chicago, catering to everyone from "the successful writer, checking information for his latest book, to the kitchenette dwelling child who stays every night until nine o'clock because there is no place at home to read or do homework."[52] At a time when access to public facilities was often limited, the Hall Branch Library provided Chicago's Black community with access to the best in literary and humanistic achievement. The library would become known for its collections, especially those relating to African American history and culture, which by the end of the 1930s were among the largest and most widely accessed in the country, second only to New York's Schomburg Center.

Behind the Hall Branch's rise to national prominence was another dedicated group of Black women, under the leadership of branch librarian Vivian G. Harsh. A woman of small stature but commanding presence, Harsh was born into the upper echelons of Black society and traced her lineage to the "Old Settlers," Black Chicagoans who had first arrived in the late nineteenth century.[53] As a result, she was well educated, attending elementary and high school in the city before receiving training at Simmons College in Boston for library sciences. By the time she took the position as head of the new Hall Branch, she was already a twenty-year veteran of the Chicago Public Libraries, its first Black employee, and its first Black branch librarian. Under the leadership of Harsh, described as "meticulous" and a "professional perfectionist," the Hall Branch library soon became the crown jewel of Chicago's Black intellectual scene.[54]

Harsh developed a range of programming at the Hall Branch, simultaneously combining "her love of and commitment to her field, with the concern for the advancement of scholarship in black areas."[55] Much like the 135th Street Branch Library in New York, which acted as an anchor for the cultural and intellectual development of Harlem during the same period, the Hall Branch in Chicago educated and connected Chicago's Black community through artistic exhibits, literary forums, speakers, and dramatic performances, creating "a space in which a people, long denied an understanding and appreciation of their own history and culture, could explore what it meant to be black."[56]

Central to this pursuit was Harsh's dedication to the work of preserving and sharing Black history. A prominent member of the ASNLH, Harsh served on the advisory committee for its 1935 meeting in Chicago. In this respect she took after Hall himself, who had been one of the four originators of the organization and served as its first president. Her zeal for engaging communities with Black culture led the Hall Branch to support the association in activities like Negro History Week, and she wove Black history into the classes, lecture forums, clubs, and exhibits the library hosted for both adults and children. As historian Anne Meis Knupfer observed, by 1944, "there were fifteen Negro History Clubs which met regularly at the Hall library and nearby schools, with over 800 persons attending the meetings."[57] Harsh also supported the development of Black history by adding extensively to the library's holdings. Utilizing a grant from the Rosenwald Foundation. Harsh traveled extensively and collected materials relating Black life, culture, and history. During her tenure with the Hall Branch this collection grew to over two thousand titles, including several rare and out-of-print manuscripts.

The small cohort of women who worked beside Harsh at the Hall Branch also supported her efforts to engage the community in Black history. At the head of this group was Charlemae Rollins, who served as the children's librarian. Rollins coordinated activities including yearly book week programs, reading guidance clinics, and children's story hours, in addition to working with teachers and parent-teacher associations at numerous area schools. Future Pulitzer Prize–winning poet Gwendolyn Brooks, who spent much of her childhood in the stacks and reading rooms of the Hall Branch, remembered Rollins's impact decades later in an unpublished handwritten poem titled "For Charlemae Rollins":

> Her gift is long delayed,
> And even now is paid,
> In insufficient measure,
> Rhymeful reverence,
> For such excellence,
> Is microscopic treasure,
> Nothing is enough,
> for one who gave us love,
> who gave us clarity,
> who gave us sentience,
> who gave us definition,
> who gave us of her vision.[58]

Like Harsh, Rollins saw part of her professional responsibility and personal mission as the spread of more full and accurate information regarding Black history. As children's librarian she made space within the Hall Branch for this work through the creation of a "Negro History Club for young people," which met at the library and was sponsored by St. Elizabeth's, one of the city's few predominantly Black Catholic schools.[59] As Rollins put it, "In trying to fit the Library Service to the needs of the children of the community, it was found that there was a need for keener awareness of the contributions of the Negro," so "teachers were invited to bring their classes (by appointment) and hear stories of Negro achievements." The Negro History

Club at the Hall Branch epitomized the close collaboration between librarians, archivists, and classroom educators, something Morgan would take full advantage of in her own work.

In addition to the appreciation hours, Rollins also dedicated time to finding reading material that depicted African Americans in realistic and unbiased ways. Faced with children's literature that often "ridiculed and caricatured the Negro child," Rollins made it her mission to stock the children's collection of the Hall Branch with material that showed African Americans "in every phase of social and economic life—books which bring him alive not only humorously, but as an earnest worker, a student, an artist, and in every natural aspect." The result of her efforts was the publication *We Build Together*, which listed and categorized positive and appropriate elementary and high school reading materials for Black youth.[60] By cataloguing these resources and making them more broadly available for use, Rollins provided critical resources to other libraries, schools, colleges, and individual educators like Morgan, who relied on the Hall Branch as a base for her research.

THE NATIONAL SORORITY OF PHI DELTA KAPPA   Not only would Morgan take advantage of the resources of the Hall Branch, not the least of which were its dedicated staff, but the library would also serve as a meeting ground for other organizations in which she participated. One of these was the National Sorority of Phi Delta Kappa, a group of Black educators who shared a common interest in promoting sisterhood among teachers and leading active campaigns on issues of child welfare. The sorority first appeared in Chicago in 1931 when midwestern regional director Mamie Brown of Charleston, West Virginia, and Rebecca Young, a transplant from Baltimore, arrived with "the expressed purpose of organizing a chapter of the sorority in the city."[61] Membership quickly grew among Chicago's Black female teachers, with the chapter serving as both a social club where Black female educators could gather to support one another and an academic organization priding itself on promoting education in the greater community. Inducted into the Mu chapter of the sorority on January 9, 1937, by 1941 Morgan had been elected to the position of local basileus, the leader of the Chicago region.

Throughout the 1930s the Mu chapter would support Black education in Chicago in numerous ways, hosting talks on educational issues and frequently publishing articles in the *Chicago Defender* dealing with new findings or campaigns. In 1936, for example, they supported Marjorie Robinson, a valedictorian of Morgan's alma mater of Englewood High School, who with their financial support became "a brilliant student at the University of Chicago."[62] The same year, the sorority also raised enough funds to provide "a two week trip to Lincoln Center Camp near Milton Junction, Wisconsin, for little Lizzette Rhone during the summer," an experience that few Black families in Chicago could afford on their own, and one that the seventh-grade Rhone was ecstatic to receive. Not surprisingly, the Mu chapter also supported the study of Black history, often partnering with other community organizations in order to do so. For instance, during its 1938 celebration of the sorority's "Better Health, Better Character" week, the Mu chapter "presented a check to the George Cleveland Hall Library, to purchase two books pertaining to Negro History."[63]

In addition to fundraising and scholarships, the organization also served as a wellspring of support for other educators. One of these educators, honored by the Mu chapter at a dinner in the late 1930s, was Maudelle Bousfield, a pioneering educator who had become the first Black principal of a Chicago school when she was assigned to head Keith Elementary in 1927, and whose husband, Midian O. Bousfield, would be appointed the first Black member of the city's board of education in 1939. As historian Dionn Danns notes, Bousfield's accomplishments were extraordinary in a school system that "barely wanted to hire Black teachers to permanent teaching posts," and as a result Bousfield enjoyed an unparallel stature and reputation among Chicago's Black educators.[64] Throughout the 1930s and 1940s Bousfield would become both a professional and personal mentor to

Morgan. As Morgan recollected in a speech at St. Edmund's Episcopal Church decades later, "In 1941 Mrs. Bousfield was the most articulate sponsor, supporter, and consultant of a program, little known but now universally accepted—Negro History. Mrs. Bousfield was my constant guide and counselor in the crucial years of 1941 and 1942." Both women agreed on the potential of Black history to spark social change, and that it should serve primarily to "give the Negro child an appreciation of his own worth and dignity as well as the worth and dignity of others."[65] Phi Delta Kappa thus facilitated connections that would be critical to the success of Morgan's later efforts.

Lastly, the Mu chapter also brought Morgan into contact with another important figure in Black history education in Chicago: Samuel B. Stratton. Speaking at a Phi Delta Kappa–sponsored event at Good Shepherd Church in 1940, Stratton echoed the words of Woodson and others by reminding his audience of parents and teachers that "the acts of Negro heroes and heroines are built into the fabric of our own nation."[66] This focus on the central place of Black people in the American story was not new for Stratton, who had organized "Know Yourself Clubs" in Chicago's Black elementary schools and sponsored Negro history clubs at Dunbar Vocational High School and DuSable High School. Born in 1897 to Congregationalist missionaries, Stratton was a career educator who began his teaching at age sixteen in a one-room, ungraded schoolhouse in the Geechee region of South Carolina. Stratton had returned to education after his service in World War I allowed him to take advantage of the Rehabilitation Act to pursue a degree at the University of Chicago, which he received in 1926. Praised by the *Chicago Defender* as the city's unofficial "dean of Black Studies," Stratton was "one of that little band of black educators who managed to instill racial pride, dignity, and respect into many, many generations of young people by making Negro history an unofficial part of the curricula."[67] Stratton's ideas meshed well with Morgan's. He shared her dedication to civic activism, including work with the NAACP, Urban League, and Kappa Alpha Psi fraternity. The two became professional allies and eventually romantic partners, marrying in 1946.

Through her relationships with the Hall Branch Library, the ASNLH, and Phi Delta Kappa, Morgan familiarized herself with the leading voices and ideas shaping an alternative black curriculum in and around Chicago. The men and women in these organizations were crucial to the work of redefining the relationship of African Americans to their history and the history of the country writ large. Moving forward she would use the inspiration she gained in these circles and add her own voice to those of individuals such as Harsh, Woodson, Stratton, Rollins, and Bousfield.

"The Study of the Negro, Accorded Its Rightful Place": Madeline Morgan Comes of Age

By the mid-1930s Madeline Morgan was an experienced educator, a progressive pedagogue, and an outspoken advocate for the teaching of Black history and culture. Like many Progressive Era educators, she held that learning was ineffectual unless it was tied to social change. As she put it, "Knowledge is power only if it is put into action."[68] However, the field of action she envisioned was beyond the interests and abilities of her white peers, and she drew instead from her personal experiences in a segregated northern city, the triumphs and disappointments of the migration era, and her determination to help end the "discrimination, restrictions, exploitations, and varied subtle and direct forms of persecution" she and others faced. If the school was to truly be the site of social regeneration, Morgan came to believe, it would have to assume "the responsibility of educating its citizens to live together in a democratic society" or continue to consign them "to live blindly and in confusion."[69]

As she turned her pedagogical training toward questions of race and history, she was nurtured by networks both formal and informal, and became part of a growing movement for Black history in Chicago's communities and classrooms. Schools were heavily implicated in the maintenance of racial prejudice, and Morgan came to believe that "the study of the Negro, accorded its rightful place in American history, will teach both sides to respect and appreciate racial diversity."[70]

For the moment, her sphere of action was limited to her small classroom at Emerson Elementary. However, as the 1930s came to an end and a new decade began, events at home and on the world stage would give Morgan the opportunity to put her theories to the test on a much greater scale.

Madeline Robinson (later Morgan), graduating from John Farren School, 1920.

CHAPTER 2

"SELF-PRESERVATION EXACTS A ONENESS IN MOTIVE AND IN DEED"

Wartime Interculturalism and the *Supplementary Units*

$\mathcal{J}$ULY 4, 1940—Four thousand attendees jostled in nervous anticipation in the dimly lit main hall of the Chicago Coliseum. For decades the stadium had played host to political conventions and sporting events, but this afternoon it opened its doors to a new kind of celebration. That summer, visitors gathered to see "an American story of achievement"—for many, nothing less than "the rebirth of a race."[1] The tension swelled as choirs sang the chords of "God Bless America," and then, finally, the moment arrived at 1:43 p.m. as "batteries of flood lights emblazoned the entire place." The president of the United States, his hand on a diamond-studded button hundreds of miles away in Hyde Park, New York, had given the signal. The American Negro Exposition, the "Negro World's Fair," had officially begun.[2]

What spectators saw when the lights went up on the exposition's main hall that afternoon was a "visual and spatial narrative of racial progress," one that brought many of the themes of the emerging Black history movement into the public sphere in new and dramatic fashion.[3] On every side of the main room, surrounding the replica of Lincoln's tomb found in the center (the exposition marked the seventy-fifth anniversary of Emancipation), were sixteen large murals and thirty-three dioramas, "spectacularly beautiful [and] historically important" which illustrated "the Negro's large and valuable contributions to the progress of America and the world." Included in the scenes were the early use of the wheel by ancient Ethiopians and the building of the Sphinx by the Egyptians, alongside more modern exploits such as the explorer Matthew Henson's journey to the North Pole, and the charge of the Buffalo Soldiers of the Tenth Cavalry at San Juan Hill during the Spanish-American War. Beyond the main hall, the exposition stretched over 52,000 square feet and contained over a hundred additional exhibits. Visitors could see the trophies won by Joe Louis, Jesse Owens, and other Black athletes; view the work of Black artists, from classical masters like Henry O. Tanner to present-day prodigies like Augusta Savage and Archibald Motley; and enjoy motion pictures and theatrical productions from writers like Arna Bontemps and Langston Hughes in the fair's four-thousand-seat theater. While walking the exposition grounds, guests heard recordings of Black music from work songs to spirituals, donated by the Columbia Record Company, pouring from the loudspeaker system throughout the day. The exposition stood in every way ready to "enlighten the world on the contributions of the Negro to civilization."[4] As one reporter commented, for twenty-five cents' admission, "a Negro couldn't purchase as much pride and glory in himself . . . anywhere in the world."[5] It was a feeling shared by many of the exposition's attendees, perhaps none more so than Madeline Morgan, the young social studies teacher from Emerson Elementary.

The American Negro Exposition was, like all works of public history, educational as well as entertaining. The event's organizers, a cross section of the middle and upper echelons of the city's Black community, sought to make it "highly educational and cultural," with "more [of] the museum than the fair aspect."[6] The result was that each of the fair's many exhibits communicated themes of pride and progress to those in attendance, both adults and the children who often accompanied them to the coliseum grounds. Black educators from schools and universities across the country counted pennies and contrived means of travel to bring their classes to tour the exhibits. Nearer to home, the Chicago Public Schools maintained a booth at the fair to communicate its own investment in Black education, while some six thousand young Black readers of the *Defender*'s Bud Billiken children's column were treated to a children's day at the exposition, which brought them into contact with the exposition and its aims while they enjoyed music, food, and shows.[7]

Morgan, like many other Black teachers, marveled to see Black history and progress represented on such a grand scale. She visited the coliseum grounds several times over the summer, becoming more enthralled with each return trip. As she put it, "I was greatly interested and impressed by the contributions that had been made by Negroes in science, health, art, and literature to American life." As a teacher, Morgan made a conscious connection between her educational work and the public history on display at the Negro World's Fair. She was fired with a passion to see that more of her students gain access to the information and perspectives the exposition contained. She began to "dream and hope for the time when Negro boys and girls would be given the opportunity to read about the achievements of our leaders and their deeds." The exposition, even with its splendid exhibits and resources, was only a temporary solution, running just sixty days in total. What Morgan needed was a means to bring the feeling of the exhibits into the classroom in a more permanent way, to fundamentally expand the curriculum her students received to reflect the contributions of Black Americans.[8]

That task would be daunting. Morgan recognized that earlier efforts to "blend Negro Achievements into the school curriculum" had "met with no success." As she began planning, she relied on the networks developed early in her career, particularly Phi Delta Kappa and the ASNLH. As she put it, "At first I thought that I would make a personal request to the Board of Education, but after thinking it over thoroughly, I decided to present the idea to the teacher's organization of which I am president. A special meeting was called and my idea of the project was submitted for discussion."[9]

After gaining the support of her fellow sorors, Morgan looked to secure help from Carter G. Woodson and the ASNLH. The sorority invited the educator and author, then in the midst of a trip to Chicago, to discuss "the various angles of the problem with us."[10] Encouraged by Woodson's endorsement and advice, the sorors created a small committee to continue to research and gather materials.

By early February 1941, only five months after the Negro World's Fair closed its doors, Morgan had marshaled enough support to put her plan into action. Relying on the collective weight of her sorority chapter and the national body of Phi Delta Kappa she crafted a letter to William H. Johnson, the superintendent of Chicago Public Schools. The first paragraph read:

A group of teachers in colored districts wish to secure your approval for an experimental project in the study of Negro history in the Chicago Public Schools. At present we celebrate Negro History Week but we feel that there is a need for a more extensive study of Negro life. Such a study will acquaint the young citizen with information concerning Negro life, will develop greater race consciousness and pride and will make the young citizen intelligent concerning his own background.[11]

Confident in her own networks and resources, Morgan stated, "Many of the teachers who favor such a plan are members of the Mu Chapter of the National Sorority of Phi Delta Kappa. . . . If you are favorably inclined toward such a proposal we will gladly plan complete units and offer a bibliography accessible to children and teachers." Morgan assured Dr. Johnson that she and her sorority were more than ready to take up the challenge should he consent to their proposal.

With her letter, Morgan sought to claim a place for Black history within Chicago's public schools and to turn the work she and others had done in individual classrooms into something larger and more lasting. The question was whether the city and its schools would be open to such change. The response would be predicated not only on Morgan's proposal but on the shifting terrain of race and representation in the larger body politic during the 1940s.

"The Hour of Peril": Chicago, the Second World War, and Interculturalism

The Second World War was a watershed moment for Black activism, organizing, and protest. Two decades before, many in the Black community had returned from the First World War hopeful that their defense of democracy on the western fronts of Europe could be translated into a similar victory over racism in United States. Those expectations had been dashed, however, as Black soldiers and their families were instead met with intensified repression and violence that led to the race riots of 1919. As Lucius Harper, an editor for the *Chicago Defender*, wrote, "We went to fight for some kind of a 'democracy' that we have never been able to understand, and we came back disillusioned, crushed, and humiliated. We got nothing but riots and unemployment for our gallantry." Now faced with the prospect of again risking themselves in service of their country, Black Americans were resolved that their sacrifices would no longer be made in vain.[12]

A wave of popular dissent, carried and expressed most vocally in the Black press, fundamentally challenged the "perversity of an American society that fought fascists and Nazis overseas in the name of freedom and justice even as it maintained segregation at home."[13] Margaret Burroughs, an artist, an educator, and a friend of Morgan's during these years, caustically asked, "Instead of wasting our men and our money on imperialist war mongers who cry 'For Democracy,' why shouldn't we utilize our men, our money, and our cultural heritage by making Democracy work in our own country?" She urged Black Americans to stand in "solid opposition to the war" until the country became "really America to BLACK AMERICANS." That mission, to force America to fulfill its historical and present-day obligation to its Black population, inspired both mass movements and individual actors throughout the war years.[14]

Black demands for equality and inclusion during the Second World War were more ardent and more aggressive than anything the country had seen before. Black Americans demanded that, whether in the armed forces, in hospitals, on factory floors, or in schools, "America give the Negro citizen the full measure of the democracy he is called on to defend."[15] This new militancy was expressed by activists spanning the full breadth of the Black community, from liberal-minded middle-class professionals like Morgan, to laborers and union leaders, to leftists, dissenters, and political radicals like Burroughs. On the streets, young African Americans like Ernest Calloway, a labor organizer in Chicago, refused to be drafted into a segregated army, declaring that he would not fight until "the defense of my country can be made on a basis of complete equality."[16] On the national level, the Committee for the Participation of Negroes in National Defense pressured the military to end its history of discrimination against Black Americans and succeeded in opening (though not in desegregating) all branches of the military to Black participation. At the same time, seeking increased opportunity on the home front, labor leader A. Philip Randolph and his March on Washington Movement fought for equal employment, forcing President Roosevelt to issue Executive Order 8802 banning discrimination in the defense industries and establishing the Fair Employment Practices Committee. As the "Double V" Campaign launched by the *Pittsburgh Courier* made clear, victory for America and its allies would be meaningful for Black people only if it signaled the defeat of both "enemies at home" and "on the battlefields abroad."[17]

As Black Americans fought for greater inclusion during the war years, white local and federal policy makers were pushed either to respond or to risk the national unity so desperately needed during wartime. The American Negro Exposition that so inspired Morgan itself showed signs of these wartime tensions. The Roosevelt administration's need to assure Black audiences that their patriotism and sacrifice were recognized had led to increased federal and state support for the exposition. The speech given by US senator James M. Slattery of Illinois, who spoke at the convention's opening, linked Black history to American progress and national defense. He began by extolling the historical contributions of Black Americans:

> We are met to bear witness to the progress of civilization. In this American Negro Exposition, which we are today dedicating to peace and understanding, we are celebrating one of the real achievements of American history. . . . None of the American miracles of our day offers stronger proof of the essential rightness of our American system than the progress of the American Negro which is celebrated and exemplified in this Exposition.[18]

Slattery's support of Black identity and culture must have seemed strange to many of the fairs' attendees. Only seven years prior the city had relegated Black participation in its Century of Progress Exposition to an ignominiously titled "Darkest Africa" concession, where patrons could pay fifty cents to watch Black dancers writhe rhythmically in mock African garb and marvel at Captain Callahan, a white man supposedly castrated at the hands of African savages in the Congo.[19] It was the lingering memory of this disenfranchisement that led Black real estate entrepreneur James W. Washington to begin planning a "Negro World's Fair" in the first place, to highlight the progress of the race since emancipation. That the resulting exposition would be opened by President Roosevelt, attended by Chicago mayor Edward Kelly, and include a speech from Senator Slattery, attested to just how momentous a shift had taken place in the intervening years. Yet the end of Slattery's speech, which focused on the Black role in the present crisis, made the goal of his paeans to Black progress more legible.

> It is fitting, too, that we should be gathered here on the Fourth of July, the birthday of freedom of all Americans. The liberties

which were proclaimed to the world as the right of Americans 164 years ago today take on new significance in this year 1940, when elsewhere in the world freedom seems about to perish from the earth.

In this hour we need for all Americans the intense patriotic devotion of the American Negro. . . . We need the unwavering loyalty of the Negroes who fought beside us in four wars before and after slavery—with Jackson in defense against the British invaders of Georgia, on a hundred bloody fields of the War between the States, with Theodore Roosevelt at San Juan hill [sic], and under Pershing on the battlefields of France.

In the hour of peril the American Negro has never failed his country. He will not fail it now.[20]

For Slattery, as for the Roosevelt administration he represented, recognition of the "progress of the American Negro" was intimately tied to the "hour of peril" the country faced and the need to secure the loyalty of Black Americans.[21] The speech, and the vision of Black history it represented, was undeniably limited, embracing Black achievement as proof of the "rightness" of the "American system" while carefully ignoring the continuing segregation, disenfranchisement, and systemic racism that belied any claim to American superiority. However, the fact that Slattery and other white officials had been forced to expend resources and adapt their rhetoric spoke to the pressure the Black community successfully exerted for "greater inclusion as full citizens" during the war years.[22] Morgan's efforts in the realm of education would mirror the significant, if incomplete, progress of the exposition.

"There Is No Greater Issue Today Before American Education": The Intercultural Education Movement

The wartime embrace of Black history and culture shown by Slattery and others, and the support of racial tolerance more broadly, would not be limited to the exposition floor in Chicago. Whether in President Roosevelt's fireside chats; the posters, pamphlets, and film reels produced by the Office of War Information; the anti-prejudice campaigns of labor unions like the Congress of Industrial Organizations (CIO); or the efforts of civic and religious bodies like the National Council of Christians and Jews, the NAACP, and the Urban League, the war was actively redefined as a struggle "not merely to defeat the nation's military enemies, but to create a more tolerant society without racial, ethnic, and religious discrimination."[23] This push, felt in the realm of politics, private industry, and community organizations, also reached the nation's schools.

As the war encompassed every part of society, schools were enlisted alongside homes and workplaces as sites of national defense. Educators joined civic, religious, and political leaders working to shore up patriotism, quell outbreaks of racial animosity, and build support for the war effort. As early as 1939, US Commissioner of Education J. D. Studebaker released an official statement in which he cited "racial and religious tolerance and understanding" as a "major problem" for American educators and proclaimed that "there is no greater issue today before American education."[24] The war had revealed not only military and political threats to the home front but ideological ones as well. As Studebaker put it:

> It would be a serious error in judgement to assume that the people of the United States must defend themselves only against the military and economic pressure of totalitarian states. It is quite as important that we strengthen the defenses of our democratic ideas against the inroads of doctrines which are so thoroughly lacking in spiritual and scientific justifications. To undertake this task is the historic duty of the schools of our nation.

In order to mount this defense, Studebaker urged "school boards, school officials, and teachers of the United States" to "give immediate attention to the problem of adapting the school curriculums and schedules to ensure the adequate and meaningful treatment of the ideas, aims, and spirit of democracy." Throughout the war, teachers, administrators, parents, and education experts around the country heeded Studebaker's call to become a "bulwark of democracy" by promoting racial and religious tolerance.[25]

Intercultural education, also called intergroup education or tolerance education, quickly became a major movement in the late 1930s and 1940s. Ideologically, it drew from several sources. Social scientists dating back to the 1920s had challenged the theories of inherent or biological difference between races that until then had lent bigotry the veneer of scientific authority. Franz Boas, for example, along with his students Ruth Benedict and Margaret Mead, had pioneered the field of cultural anthropology by arguing that racial and ethnic differences previously ascribed to biology were instead the result of culture. This central idea was disseminated by Boas both within and outside of the academy through speeches, scientific studies, books, and newspaper and journal articles. Building on the work of Benedict, Boas, and Mead, organizations including the Council Against Intolerance in America and the National Conference of Christians and Jews emerged during the 1920s and 1930s and worked to spread this new understanding of race and culture. As "the spread of racism in Germany inspired efforts to counter racism at home," these groups saw their arguments met with even wider acceptance.[26]

While Boas, Mead, and Benedict provided the scientific underpinnings of tolerance education by outlining a new understanding of race and difference, the movement that most directly shaped how interculturalism looked in primary and secondary schools was the cultural gifts model developed by educator and social activist Rachel Davis DuBois. DuBois, who founded the Service Bureau for Education in Human Relations in 1934 (later the Service Bureau for Intercultural Education), originally developed her program in anti-prejudice education during the 1920s as a response to the nativism and xenophobia she had seen directed against minorities, especially white ethnic immigrants, as a teacher in Woodbury, New Jersey. A fervent pacifist, she believed that the key to peace both nationally and internationally was the appreciation of difference. This appreciation could be accomplished by the "spread of accurate knowledge concerning the ideals, traditions, and experience of other peoples," which would lead to greater empathy and understanding between cultural groups.[27] For DuBois, learning about the contributions of racial and religious minorities would lead to increased tolerance between groups.

During the war years, these preexisting anti-prejudice education movements would receive greater attention and a greatly expanded audience. As historian Zoe Burkholder writes, "At the outbreak of war professional educators seized the cultural gifts movement, and with minor modifications, held it up as the most promising strategy to reduce racial tensions through public education."[28] Teachers and administrators across the country experimented with lessons, assemblies, plays, and pageants meant to increase intercultural understanding. While white educators tended to focus on European immigrant communities, some also included units on African Americans alongside their discussions of Polish, Italian, and Russian Jewish contributions. Beyond this, many Black teachers also used interculturalism as an entry point to discuss democratic ideals and racial equality.

The reach of interculturalism grew during the war years, becoming a national movement. The radio program *Americans All, Immigrants All*, a twenty-six-part series that aired from November 1938 to May 1939, exemplified the popularity of tolerance education outside of the schoolhouse doors. Developed by the US Office of Education in conjunction with the Service Bureau for Intercultural Education and the Columbia Broadcasting System (CBS), the series was designed to "promote a more appreciative understanding of our growing American culture through the dramatization of the contributions made by the different groups which are a part of it."[29] Each week on Sundays, at 2:00 p.m. Eastern Standard Time, listeners were led through the experience of a particular racial, ethnic, or religious group in episodes like "Our Hispanic Heritage," "The Negro," and "Near Eastern People," meant to "dramatize the contribution of racial minorities to the greatness of the United States."[30] Hailed as a massive success by critics from all corners, *Americans All, Immigrants All* drew huge listening audiences, and over eighty thousand individual pieces of mail were sent to the Office of Education in response to the series.[31] The program received awards from groups like the Women's National Radio Committee, which represented twenty-four national women's organizations with over ten million members, who deemed it "the most original and informative program" to air on radio that year.[32] This impact was extended further by the production of listening guides for teachers and students that allowed the program to be used in classrooms across the nation.

Although broadly popular, series like *Americans All* also showed the serious limitations of intercultural education as a vehicle for racial justice. Since the overriding goal was to promote a sense of patriotism and common purpose, and the main audience was students from the majority group who would ostensibly be taught to respect and tolerate difference, the series avoided uncomfortable or problematic topics such as racial segregation. Instead, the seamless integration of immigrant and minority groups into a prosperous and powerful American whole was emphasized. The episode dedicated to "The Negro in American Life," which aired nationwide on December 11, 1938, provides one example. The episode was praised by the Black press, including the *Defender*, for sharing the "impressive contributions members of the Race have made to the culture and welfare of the United States," including information on historical figures such as Booker T. Washington, Jan Matzeliger, and Crispus Attucks. However, these substantive sections were diminished by other portions that fell back on well-worn stereotypes. Discussion questions posed to young audiences in the reading guide that accompanied the episode, for instance, asked students to "name what you think is the Negro's greatest gift to American life—his labor, folktales, dances, songs, or his cheerfulness?" Even more disconcerting, while the episode provided a positive image of Black history in the United States, it offered little comment on the current state of Black American disenfranchisement.

"Applied to the Negro Question Today, Tolerance . . . May Mean Almost Anything": Black Educators and Interculturalism

The hesitancy of white proponents of tolerance education to deal openly with issues of racial inequality was often critiqued by Black teachers, who questioned the commitment of their newfound allies to promoting true equality. A 1945 article in the *Negro History Bulletin* recognized that "during these days of much talk about tolerance much interest has been expressed in the Negro." However, while for the moment there seemed to be no end to the "many whites who desired to stage public demonstrations of the accomplishments of the Negroes," the authors worried that "such interest is often spasmodic and may not deepen into a sustained effort to change a social attitude of long standing."³³ An article written a year earlier in the same publication questioned the motives of tolerance organizations, whose lack of clear stances on structural issues such as discrimination in housing and education meant that "applied to the Negro question, tolerance . . . may mean almost anything."³⁴ The authors of this piece decided that in the end what was needed were "not so many agencies to fight intolerance, but more aggressive organizations to deal drastically with those who are opposed to the principles of the United States Constitution." Black educators realized that in the absence of dedication to amending racist institutions, education alone would do little to bring about the changes they ultimately sought.

As these articles made clear, the goals of Black educators went far beyond a thin commitment to building intercultural understanding. As historian Jonna Perrillo has written, "For blacks in the 1940s, school reform was part of a larger agenda that would regulate equal access and treatment in the military, employment, and housing. For white liberals, however . . . race reform depended first and foremost on improving individual and communal relationships between blacks and whites."³⁵ However, even as Black educators recognized the limits of the tolerance education movement, many believed it a useful, if imperfect, tool. Throughout the war Black educators mobilized the rhetoric of equality embedded in the wartime tolerance movement to strengthen their own calls for inclusion. Ambrose Caliver, the pioneering Black educator and senior specialist with the US Office of Education, endorsed the use of the schools to "improve human relations and develop racial tolerance." Critical to this mission, Caliver argued, was the need to "emphasize the contributions of each race and group to the advancement of our civilization, and the oneness of our purpose in assuring freedom for all."[36] Likewise, historian Lawrence Reddick, called on the government to support national unity through "the developing of a positive program of diffusing the truth about Negroes and Negro life," which would fight racist propaganda by highlighting "the scientists, scholars, artists—all those who have made a distinct contribution to American and world culture."[37]

Echoing this sentiment, the NAACP released the pamphlet *Anti-Negro Propaganda in Textbooks* (1939), which used the language of wartime tolerance as ammunition to launch a broadside against racism in school materials, a problem they had long contended with. The authors began by describing the "crimes being perpetrated upon the children of Europe," where "race hatred" and "intolerance" had been allowed to "choke the fine flower of fresh, eager, and growing minds." They then turned to the United States and charged that the same "false race theories" that had given rise to fascist regimes abroad had been allowed to fester in American schoolbooks in the form of histories that spread "false conceptions about the Negro people and their relationship to their fellow citizens." Although the NAACP had waged similar campaigns over school texts for decades, the authors remarked that the need to correct the depiction of Black Americans was especially pressing "at a time when democracy is being assailed as never before" and that "a full phase of this fight must be directed against those who would deny to the Negro citizens of America their rightful place . . . among the pioneers who have laid the foundation and helped develop our country." Like Caliver, the NAACP used the war to urge the expansion of the curriculum to include Black historical achievement.[38]

The argument that racial intolerance propagated by the schools was a danger not just to US society but also to the war effort was picked up by Black leaders and white allies in Chicago as well. Albert Beckham, a member of the Chicago Board of Education, the third Black American to earn a doctorate in psychology, and the first Black school psychologist in the nation, argued that the energies of Chicago's Black children were necessary to America's war effort, as "America needs her youth—white youth, black youth, and all other youth." However, meeting the challenge of engaging youth in the war effort would mean casting off outdated patterns of thought and representation. Critically, the young Black people's commitment to the defense of democracy could not live in "the midst of Jim Crowism and racial antipathy." Beckham's answer, like that of Caliver, Reddick, and the NAACP, was education. As he put it, "This country might well consider a program of developing war attitudes among Negro children and youth" that would "permit the Negro an equal part in the struggle abroad and human rights at home." Beckham may not have known it at the time, but just such a program had been put into place months earlier in his own backyard.[39]

A small number of influential white Chicagoans also took up the call for racial tolerance. Bernard J. Sheil, an outspoken Catholic bishop, became a dedicated advocate of tolerance education and racial equality during the war years. Sheil agreed with Black activists that it was "the most dangerous kind of hypocrisy to wage a war for democracy and at the same time to deny the basic benefits of democracy to any group of citizens," and he urged white parishioners to decide whether they would rather "save their pride and privileges or save their country."[40] Already pursuing interculturalism through the Catholic Youth Organization, whose intramural sports competitions brought Black and white youth into friendly competition and contact, Sheil expanded his efforts through the establishment of the Sheil School of Social Studies. Begun in 1943, the school was tuition free and open to all, regardless of race or class, an experiment in adult instruction that focused on the social, economic, and political education of working-class Chicagoans. The topics covered, from "The History of Race Prejudice in America" to "Reconstructing the Social Order" to "Problems of a Wartime Economy," revealed the strong social justice commitments of what Sheil referred to as the "labor school." Many of Chicago's most prominent Black educators were part of the integrated faculty, including Morgan, who taught courses in "Negro History" that paralleled to the work she pursued with Chicago's school-age youth.[41]

Both Black educators and white liberal allies, in Chicago and nationally, endorsed the intercultural education movement. The Second World War created opportunities for Black educators to "discuss the defining principles of democracy, the civil rights of all citizens, and the dangers of racial discrimination in a way that would have been impossible a few years earlier."[42] Morgan would navigate this newly created discursive space within the Chicago schools.

"Self-Preservation Exacts a Oneness in Motive and in Deed":
Wartime Tolerance and the Supplementary Units

The war effort and the intercultural education movement formed the backdrop against which Superintendent Johnson received the letter from Madeline Morgan and her sorority in the early spring of 1941. The war had impacted every aspect of education in Chicago, from the structure of the school day to the content of individual courses. As Johnson put it, "War makes exacting demands upon the resources, the capacities, and the efficiency of every course in the curriculum of the American schools. There is not a subject that has escaped the challenge to change its pattern, to conform to the emergency, and to help solve the problems of production." As a result, Chicago Public Schools adopted a policy of experimentation, encouraging teachers to "try out suggested classroom improvements, or to propose entirely new ideas for the common good of educational progress." As part of this shift Johnson had embraced elements of wartime interculturalism as part of the war effort, communicated through radio broadcasts, instructions to teachers and administrators, and monthly Americanism bulletins that sought to reinforce the "obligation of tolerance of race, religion, opinion, and custom, which is imposed by the Constitution of the United States." An experiment in Black history like the one suggested by Morgan appealed to Johnson's wartime mindset and goals.[43]

On March 25, 1941, at 4:30 p.m., Madeline Morgan was invited to meet with Superintendent Johnson to discuss her proposed plan. The meeting must have been an interesting one. At forty-six, Johnson was the older of the pair by eleven years, a white man in a position of authority over one of the nation's largest school systems. Yet, if these facts threatened to erode Morgan's confidence, she had her own strengths to rely on. She was meticulously organized and her ideas were well planned. She was an experienced educator and an active leader and organizer with significant organizational backing. She also possessed a familiarity navigating white institutional spaces, gained from her experiences at Englewood High School, the Chicago Normal College, and Northwestern University, the last of which happened also to be the alma mater of the man she now sat across from.

No record exists of the initial conversation between Johnson and Morgan, but it was evidently successful because the next day at 3:00 p.m. a second conversation occurred. This meeting included not just Morgan and Johnson but also Morgan's principal, Elinor C. McCollom, and Mary G. Lusson, the director of the Bureau of Curriculum for the school district. It was at this second meeting that a more formal plan of action began to take shape. Morgan would construct a curriculum guide that followed the normal course of study for grades K–8 but included material on Black contributions that had hitherto been excluded. To create the space and time for Morgan to complete this work, Johnson transferred her from the classroom to an office at the Bureau of Curriculum. Her new position would give her access to additional resources, including her choice of a research assistant to aid in the work. For this task, Morgan enlisted Bessie S. King, a teacher at nearby Betsy Ross Elementary School. The choice of King as a coworker reveals Morgan's continued reliance on networks of support within the Black community. As she stated in an internal letter to her

Phi Delta Kappa sorority sisters, when given the opportunity to pick her assistant, there was simply no choice: "Of course I chose a soror." An oversight committee was also formed that included McCollom, principal Lois Morstrom of Betsy Ross Elementary, and Ruth Jackson, principal of Colman Elementary and the only African American elementary school principal in Chicago at that time. While the committee oversaw the production of the new units of study, Morgan and King were given "all the freedom necessary to complete the research work."[44]

On March 31, 1941, King and Morgan officially began their research. We know relatively little about the process, as Morgan left few details of the day-to-day work. However, we do know that the pair was dedicated, scouring multiple sources to fact-check every point, writing different authors and experts to follow up on incomplete or unclear information, working into the night and over weekends, and making use of local resources like the Art Institute of Chicago and the Field Museum. Unsurprisingly, their research also brought Morgan and King back into the stacks and reading rooms of the Hall Branch Library, whose extensive collections on African and African American life and culture provided critical sources of information. Throughout the war, Chicago's public libraries engaged in various efforts to bridge racial and ethnic divides, creating reading lists on intercultural education and minority contributions, and Morgan and King's project fit well within the Hall Branch's larger wartime mission. Librarian Marian Hadley, for example, created a pamphlet titled *Negro Soldiers in American Wars* and compiled slide footage of Black soldiers that was utilized by local schools, while children's librarian Charlemae Rollins authored *We Build Together*, a "handbook to Negro life and literature" used by several library branches and in some schools. As Rollins noted, Morgan's project was just one of the wartime initiatives located at the Hall Branch: "Out of the outstanding activities in which the entire staff was able to participate was the recent project of the Chicago Board of Education. Superintendent William Johnson released two Negro teachers from classroom duty last year to prepare a Course of Study in Negro History to be included in the curriculum of the Chicago Schools. These teachers worked at the library with the books and librarians all year."[45]

The extent to which the library proved a vital source to Morgan and King's research can be seen in the final version of the curriculum. In the second-grade materials, the authors choose the Hall Branch as a setting.[46] The inclusion of the library and of Charlemae Rollins as a character showed the gratitude and respect Morgan and King felt for the library and its staff, and also invited potential readers, both white and Black, to visit the library for themselves and take part in the story hours and readings they heard described in the units.

As the project progressed, Morgan and King also looked for additional outside expertise, submitting the materials to academics whose work centered on race, including Carter G. Woodson, Northwestern University anthropologist Melville Herskovits, University of Chicago historian Avery O. Craven, and Charles H. Wesley, the president of Wilberforce University. These figures lent not only their expertise but also their stature and credibility to the project.

Equally important, Morgan and King also worked to ensure that the curriculum they created met with the approval of educators and students by sending them to Maudelle Bousfield and Ruth Jackson, the city's lone black principals at the high school and elementary school levels, respectively, as well as to a group of "outstanding colored teachers," including Clara Anderson and Samuel Stratton of DuSable High School and Thelma Powell of Wendell Phillips High School, both bastions of Black education famed for the quality of their teaching. Finally, the finished units were tested through school visits to "observe [student] reactions, interests, and vocabulary difficulties." This feedback, along with that of experts and educators, was incorporated into the curriculum as King and Morgan moved toward completing their work. What emerged from this process of research, correspondence, writing, testing, and rewriting was a set of materials unlike any then in use in Chicago's social studies classrooms. Through the use of biographical passages, short stories, poems, and musical recordings, Morgan and King showed the African American presence in the central events of US history. As the authors stated in their foreword addressed to teachers and students, "it is the purpose of this material to show that the Negro has made and is still making his contribution to American life."

By the spring of 1942, the units Morgan had devised, titled *Supplementary Units for the Course of Instruction in Social Studies: The Negro in American Life*, were ready for classroom use. The new curriculum was unveiled at 2:00 p.m. on Thursday, May 28, 1942, at Emerson Elementary, the school Madeline had left to begin her curricular efforts a year earlier, in a ceremony that involved not only the board of education but also an audience "consisting of leaders interested in the field of Negro education." Johnson himself took the opportunity to report on the "work of the committee" whose "function it was to make a study of the achievements of the Negro and his contributions to American life." Morgan and King, along with the three principals chosen to oversee the project, were also on hand and "prepared to answer questions concerning their work."[47]

In explaining the curriculum and its significance, Superintendent Johnson invoked the language of intercultural education. In an article published in the *Defender* in fall of 1942, for example, Johnson justified the *Supplementary Units* by appealing to the themes of democracy, tolerance, and American exceptionalism. Johnson stated that "the public schools of our nation are the training ground for the development of understanding and tolerance toward all people who make up our great democracy, people of all races and religious creeds, people of all nations."[48] For Black students, he saw the units as a source of racial pride and patriotism. The material presented would show that "the Negro is serving his country today, and will be ready and willing to serve it in the future as the need arises." Indeed, much of Johnson's article focused on the theme of Black military participation and the "splendid record" of Black soldiers and seamen in the First World War.

For white students, on the other hand, Johnson believed the material would foster understanding and acceptance of their Black neighbors. This too, in Johnson's logic, was tied to the war effort and the need for a unified front that included all Americans. The connection between Black history, racial tolerance, and the war effort was made explicit in a passage from a board of education report outlining curricular changes brought on by the war effort:

> The current struggle demands that America use all of its human and natural resources. This in turn requires that a total unity never before perpetuated in this free country be perpetuated. The social studies are teaching that there is no place for pettiness and intolerance of race, religion, or politics. Self-preservation exacts a oneness in motive and in deed. Illustrative of this point are the Supplementary Units for the Course of Study in Social Studies, published in 1942, which are devoted to the contributions of the American Negro to the cultural life of the nation.[49]

Johnson related the ideas of tolerance, patriotism, and interracial cooperation in a manner consistent with political figures like Roosevelt and Slattery and educators such as Studebaker.

Interest Convergence and Black Advancement

Between the American Negro Exposition in 1940 and the completion of the *Supplementary Units* in 1942, Morgan brought her plan to incorporate Black history into the curriculum of the Chicago schools from idea to reality. Her success was a result of her ambition and dedication, but also a reflection of larger social and political contexts, including the national movement for intercultural education taken up in various forms by leaders in Chicago and across the country.

Superintendent Johnson's support of Morgan and her calls for curricular reform might best be understood as an example of what critical race theorists term "interest convergence," a concept first introduced by legal scholar Derrick Bell, who posited that advances for Black rights have historically been "accommodated only when that interest converges with the interests of whites in policy making positions."[50]

While he argues that the passage of the Emancipation Proclamation and the Reconstruction-era amendments to the Constitution protecting Black citizenship both provide examples of this principle at work, his most compelling example is the *Brown v. Board of Education* ruling that ended federal support for educational segregation. Questioning the standard interpretation of the *Brown* case as a milestone on America's "long, slow, but always uphill" journey toward equality, Bell recasts the decision as a Cold War policy move meant to burnish America's reputation in its war against communism abroad. Drawing on documents from the press, the US State Department, and elsewhere, Bell shows that "while nowhere mentioned in the Supreme Court's *Brown* opinion, a major motivation for outlawing racial segregation in 1954, as opposed to the many failed opportunities in the past, was the major boost that this decision provided in our competition with communist governments abroad and the campaign to uproot subversive elements at home."[51] Although, as Bell insists, the role of the NAACP and grassroots protesters working throughout the 1930s and 1940s cannot be discounted, the *Brown* decision would not have occurred without an external threat that drew the interests of the Black community and those of white policy makers into alignment. White self-interest, then, was the "necessary prerequisite to racial reform."[52]

Similarly, in the 1930s and 1940s, Black dissent threatened to impede America's ability to successfully prosecute the war abroad, leading to a strengthening of the position of Black activists in battles over labor, civil rights, and education at home. In each of these areas, white policy makers, acting out of a convergence of interests, were moved to grant concessions that would not have been necessary in other circumstances. Part of this process involved a change in rhetoric and representation around race, and the creation of a movement for tolerance and unity that impacted politics, popular discourse, and pedagogy.

Morgan's effort came at a moment when the demands of Black educators and their liberal white allies received a larger and more receptive hearing than they had previously been afforded. This reality gave her the opportunity to seize the attention and resources of the nation's second-largest school system and put them to work in service of Black history and culture. It would also, however, constrain the type of curriculum she could ultimately develop, as her work would need to fit within the bounds of wartime Americanism and interculturalism. Lastly, because her curriculum was tied to the war effort, Morgan would see her plans threatened in the postwar era as new sets of interests came into play. For the moment, however, the war had created an opportunity to push the Black history movement toward broader recognition, and Morgan was just the person to claim it.

CHAPTER 3

"A WORTHY PIECE OF WORK"

The *Supplementary Units* as Alternative
Black Curriculum

$\mathcal{M}$AY 19, 1942—Days before the official unveiling of the *Supplementary Units* at Emerson Elementary, and a little over a year after her research with Chicago Public Schools' Bureau of Curriculum began, Madeline Morgan wrote to her sorors in Phi Delta Kappa to announce that the curriculum she had envisioned in the hallways of the 1940 American Negro Exposition was finally complete. As her letter made clear, the adoption of the new curriculum was a unique undertaking. As Morgan wrote: "I am deeply grateful to Dr. Johnson and Miss Mc-Collom for having given us such an opportunity. . . . Nowhere in the United States has such a project been authorized for city-wide study. Such a study will not only serve as a source of inspiration to Negro youth but as information for youth in general." Because of the marked nature of the project, Morgan encouraged her sorority sisters to write from across the country in a show of support: "I beg of you to send letters and telegrams on or before May 28 to Dr. Johnson and Miss McCollom. I hope their offices will be flooded with telegrams and letters of race appreciation." In addition, the sorority would also send official communications to noted leaders in education and civil rights, including "the President of the United States, Mrs. Roosevelt, Mrs. Bethune, Marian Anderson, Paul Robeson and many others," to make them aware of the events transpiring in the Chicago schools.[1]

Morgan ended her missive by enjoining her sisters to remain quiet and coordinated in their efforts until the proper time. She urged them as a "special request" to "give this project no paper publicity until after May 28." Morgan knew that much would depend on the reception her work received when it became public. Her final line offered up a nervous but hopeful plea: "Pray that we do a worthy piece of work on May 28."[2]

Even a brief reading of the curriculum that Morgan and King authored shows that their efforts indeed amounted to "a worthy piece of work."[3] From the selection of source material to the content of the biographies, poems, stories, nonfiction passages, prompts for discussion, and suggested activities that the units' 127 pages comprised, Morgan and King reframed both world and US history in order to embrace the perspectives of the emerging alternative Black curriculum, a "pedagogical counter narrative" meant to "provide a more accurate rendering of US and world history."[4] Central to this reframing were several key arguments, emphasizing the importance of Africa to world history; linkages between African cultures and the New World; the participation of Black people in the exploration and settlement of the Americas; slavery as a system of violence and exploitation fought against by both Black activists and enlightened white allies; the bravery and heroism of Black Americans who engaged in military service throughout the nation's history; the incredible progress of Black people nationally in the modern era; and the prominent place of the Black community in the local history of Chicago. Throughout the curriculum, Morgan and King emphasized Black agency and autonomy in shaping significant events in national and world history. The *Supplementary Units* offered a counternarrative to white-authored curricula of the time, one that revealed a commitment to a new vision of American history.

One of the first ways in which the *Supplementary Units* signaled a break from the dominant historical narrative was in the selection of sources. Morgan and King referenced and carefully cited other Black scholars who articulated a new narrative of America's past. The books most often referenced were Carter G. Woodson's foundational texts *The Negro in Our History, Negro Makers of History* (which covered the same material at a more accessible elementary level), and *The Story of the Negro Retold.* Morgan and King also drew from other texts including *A Short History of the American Negro* and *Negro Builders and Heroes,* both authored by Benjamin Brawley, a dean at Morehouse College, and *An Elementary History of America Including the Contributions of the Negro Race* written by Merl Eppse, the chair of social studies and professor of history at A & I State College in Nashville, and A. P. Foster of the Tennessee Historical Society. The incorporation of these sources showed their connection to the larger "counter canon" produced by Black historians and their allies.[5]

In addition to the book-length manuscripts from academics, Morgan and King relied on several periodicals and academic journals to make their historical arguments. The *Journal of Negro History,* the mouthpiece for Woodson's ASNLH, and the *Negro History Bulletin,* the organization's offshoot for K–12 educators and their students, were both prominently featured. The *Journal of Negro Education,* published by Howard University, and *Phylon: The Clark Atlanta University Review of Race and Culture,* were both quoted throughout the *Supplementary Units.* Popular publications like the NAACP's *Crisis* and the National Urban League's *Opportunity: A Journal of Negro Life* also found their way into Morgan and King's work. Actively involved in the NAACP, Urban League, and ASNLH, Morgan most likely had a deep familiarity with these publications and brought this knowledge to bear as she constructed her curriculum.

The choice of source material by Morgan and King is significant in two ways. First, it allowed the authors to self-consciously position themselves as part of the larger intellectual project of the alternative Black curriculum, which worked to produce "historical studies, textbooks, journal articles, and encyclopedias with the sole intent of challenging the prevailing anti-Black ideologies of science and history."[6]

Moreover, Morgan and King were among the first to place such material in front of both Black and white students in a major metropolitan school district with the support of the Black community and the city's white educational establishment. As such, they opened a new front in the battle to bring Black history to a wider audience.

Second, the *Supplementary Units* introduced readers, both students and teachers, to this new body of literature on the Black experience. The units included detailed bibliographies and resources for teachers, along with further suggested readings for students. In this way, they challenged what constituted legitimate sources of historical knowledge and encouraged others to do the same.

"Thrilling Happenings in the Lives of the African People": *Reclaiming Africa*

Within the *Supplementary Units*, Morgan and King worked to directly address the negative discourses surrounding Black identity. The first means of achieving this goal was to challenge Western representations of the African continent and its peoples. The Africa of European and American popular culture was a distorted image, refracted through dime-store novels, Tarzan films, and the memoirs of missionaries and game hunters. A foreboding landscape filled with "impenetrable jungles, wild beasts, savage men, and primitive governments," this imagined Africa was seen as disconnected from the major currents of world history and largely ignored by white textbook authors.[7]

However, even as African history and culture were discounted in popular culture and the academy, Black Americans maintained a distinct connection to the continent as "the sense that African Americans shared a history with Africans and all peoples of African descent had long been an important part of African American thought."[8] This connection flowered in the early and mid-twentieth century with the emergence of a range of Pan-Africanist political and intellectual projects. Organizations spanning the ideological spectrum called for strengthened connections to the continent during these decades, from the more moderate NAACP and National Urban League to the early

Black feminist International Council of Women of the Darker Races and National Council of Negro Women, to Marcus Garvey's politically populist United Negro Improvement Association, to religious movements like the emerging Nation of Islam. Each of these groups encouraged African Americans, including children and youth, to embrace their African heritage in new ways. In addition, events on the world's stage, including Ethiopia's struggle to remain the last independent African republic after its invasion by Mussolini's Italy in 1935, brought the continent into the mainstream of Black American consciousness. The events that led to the Second World War in particular prompted Black Americans to connect their own struggle for citizenship to anti-colonial and independence movements elsewhere around the globe as "Black America's relationship with Africa existed not in a vacuum but in a world of rising fascism, world war, superpower rivalry, and an emerging third world."[9]

The early Black history movement added to these intellectual currents and brought them to younger audiences. The NAACP's *Brownies' Book*, the "first major periodical for Black children," incorporated stories on current events and African history beside proverbs, riddles, and folktales from the continent.[10] Black-authored textbooks also extolled the African past. Woodson's *African Heroes and Heroines* and *Negro Makers of History* each offered a survey of African history before the slave trade in order to illustrate the fact that Africans "had advanced far in civilization before the Europeans came to their continent" and that they "had a mode of living that was suitable to their environment and in harmony with their own way of seeing and understanding the things about them."[11] While Woodson and others offered counterpoints, however, most textbooks still approached the continent with a mix of sensationalism and pseudoscience. As Woodson observed wryly in his *African Heroes and Heroines*, "neither Europeans nor Americans, as a rule, endeavor to tell the truth about Africa."[12] Morgan and King, like other writers of the alternative Black curriculum, would approach their task in ways that sought to consciously "redefine Africa and reestablish its significance in the lives of African Americans."[13]

In white-authored textbooks, Africa was treated as insignificant to world history. While a few writers included brief sections on Egypt, which was falsely categorized as Western because of its connection to the ancient Greeks, coverage of other African civilizations was by and large nonexistent. Textbooks such as *America's Roots in the Past* by Daniel J. Beeby, *The Story of Our Country* by Ruth and Willis Mason West, and *Exploring American History* by Mabel B. Casner and Ralph Henry Gabriel, each approved and used in the Chicago Public Schools during the 1930s and 1940s, failed to include Africa at all. Instead, Western European culture, customs, and history were presented in isolation. Beeby, for example, a principal at Oglesby Elementary School in Chicago, began his textbook with the confident assertion that "the history of our civilization began... in Europe" and that the major task of American history was to "discover, if we can, what it inherited from its European parents and grandparents."[14] In order to trace this cultural inheritance, Beeby included chapters such as "The Feudal System," "The Roman Empire," and "How the Greeks Became the Teachers of the World," followed by discussion questions, the first of which was "What can we Americans learn about our own civilization by studying the history of Europe?"[15]

The Story of Our Country also framed America as an extension of European civilization. The book's first unit, titled "Europe Finds a New World," included sections on ancient Greece, Rome, and medieval Europe, culminating in a chapter in which "The White Man Finds America." Thus, from the outset, American history was deemed synonymous with the history of Western Europe and its descendants. Africa and peoples of African descent are kept well outside of the historical frame.[16]

The marginalization of Africa and its history was harmful in several ways. Through omission, textbooks like these promoted the idea that Africa was a place devoid of civilization and culture, a dark continent with no importance to the historical record. Since these materials argued that Africa held no tradition worthy of recognition, it followed that African Americans possessed no culture of their own, beyond the slavery and oppression experienced in the New World. This logic not only legitimated the historical exploitation of Black people in America and elsewhere but also reinforced their continued political and legal subjugation in the present. In the sections dedicated to Africa in the *Supplementary Units*, Morgan and King worked to counteract these negative effects by situating Africa within world history and drawing connections between Africans and their descendants in America and around the globe.

Because the absence of Africa from the historical record left African Americans as a "history-less people," reclaiming the continent was one of the most crucial tasks for the historians engaged in creating the alternative Black curriculum.[17] Morgan and King begin their unit on the continent by addressing the persistence of the dark continent myth, stating: "Often we speak of Africa as the dark continent. For many years it was the dark continent because it was not known. It was the land of mystery—a land of terror and black magic."[18] They then challenge this rendering of Africa as one based on ignorance and incomplete knowledge: "Now we know better. Explorers have traveled all over Africa. They tell us of the beautiful things they have seen; of gorgeously feathered birds, of strange and brilliant flowers, and of deep blue lakes. Historians tell us of thrilling happenings in the lives of the African people."

Importantly, Morgan and King root their appeal in the language of objective research and scientific observation. In *Negro Makers of History*, Woodson similarly explained that "we do not yet know much of Africa; but what we have recently learned about Africans has convinced *thinking people* [emphasis mine] that they are not inferior to other races, as thoughtless persons sometimes say."[19] In both cases this rhetorical move asserted the appropriate recognition of Africa as a product of scientific consensus and enlightened observation, against the uninformed and negative portrayals of previous accounts.

After deconstructing the myth of the "dark continent," Morgan and King provide students with information on Africa, both its historical contributions and its current position in world affairs. Lessons on Africa appear in the materials for third and sixth grades within the *Supplementary Units*. In both cases, most of the descriptive material is given to the kingdom of Dahomey, in what is now Benin, on the West African coast. By focusing on this region, Morgan and King are able to draw connections between the peoples of West Africa and their descendants in the New World and argue that African Americans deserve to be as proud of their heritage as any other racial or ethnic group.

The slaves who were taken from West Africa are the forefathers of the American Negro. There are many Europeans who came to America to live. All of them know something about their ancestors and the countries from which they came. They are justly proud of their heritage. However, for so long Africa was the dark continent, little was known about the lives of the ancestors of the American Negro. Now that more is known we can learn more about them.[20]

By tracing the connection between West Africa and America, Morgan and King put themselves at the forefront of a newly emerging academic consensus. A year before Morgan and King's curriculum appeared in Chicago's schools, Melville Herskovits, an anthropologist at Northwestern University and one of the experts who served on the advisory panel for the *Supplementary Units*, released his groundbreaking *The Myth of the Negro Past*. Building off the foundations laid by Du Bois, Woodson, and others, Herskovits challenged the notion that slavery had left Black Americans without a cultural lineage and provided new historical and anthropological evidence that West African religious, social, and artistic practices had not only survived but continued to influence Black Americans and other Black peoples throughout the diaspora in the present. Studying these cultural and historical links was important, Herskovits asserted, because to provide the Black reader with "an appreciation of his past" was to "endow him with the confidence in his own position in this country and in the world," built on "a foundation of scientific fact."[21] Additionally, Herskovits thought that such knowledge, "diffused over the population as a whole," would lead to "a lessening of interracial tensions" as white audiences were forced to replace myths about Black people with historical realities.

Morgan and King's material on Dahomey and other West African nations echoes Herskovits's insistence that African history and culture were the necessary starting point for any discussion of Black American history and culture. In addition, they share Herskovits's concern with using this new understanding of Africa and its connections to the global diaspora as a tool for increasing Black pride and reducing anti-Black prejudice. Throughout the war years Herskovits not only supported the *Supplementary Units* but also participated in efforts like the Council Against Intolerance in America's 1940 conference themed "Tolerance through Education" and spoke to teachers' groups in Chicago and nationally concerning the tolerance movement.

In their descriptions of Dahomey, the *Supplementary Units* form a picture of a complex and advanced society. Students are told that order is maintained by a "strong central government headed by a king and his court," that towns and villages are maintained with markets, shrines, temples, and houses connected by wide, clean streets, and that the economy is organized around agricultural production and a system of trade guilds for such occupations as weaving and metalwork.[22] The epitome of this organized and highly efficient society is found in the city of Benin, which Morgan and King tell readers has become famous for its "art and high degree of civilization." The Beni, a "pure Negro tribe," are responsible for the creation of a city with walls "ten feet high," streets lined with "well constructed houses," and impressive "colonnades of wooden pillars" covered in "bronze plaques showing battle scenes." The image of Dahomey overall is a land of incredible natural wealth, political advancement, and cultural attainment.[23]

Although Morgan and King spend most of their time on Dahomey, they also survey the accomplishments of several ancient and medieval African empires, which they refer to collectively as the "old kingdoms." These include the city-states of Timbuktu and Jenne, which, readers learn, were seats of learning whose influence stretched "throughout northern African, Spain, and the Near East." In response to the dominant narrative that Africa had given nothing of value to the Western world, Morgan and King give evidence that "these old kingdoms and cities influenced the civilization of the ancient world" through their connections with peoples in southern Europe and throughout the Mediterranean. Morgan and King also describe the Ashanti Empire, detailing the rich and vibrant life within its many towns and urban centers, its advanced political and economic systems, and its highly developed cultural life. Readers are told that the riches of the Ashanti were such that the first Europeans who witnessed them were speechless and "gazed with astonishment at the gorgeous silk umbrellas, the thousands of soldiers, the beautiful silken robes of the attendants, and the skillfully made swords, canes, and jewelry of pure gold."[24]

Significantly, Morgan and King inform readers that although these African kingdoms had fallen to European colonization, they had not altogether vanished. Instead, the splendor of these cultures remained, as even "under European control . . . Africans keep much of their own way of living and governing."[25] This point was especially meaningful at a time when the Second World War had "unleashed an array of anticolonial challenges and accelerated the crumbling of European hegemony."[26] If Africa had not lost its culture under foreign rule, students could imagine the continent reborn in a post-colonial world.

Morgan and King do not only address lies and distortions about the advancement of African societies; they also work to counter negative assumptions about the character and capacity of Africans as people. Popular representations portrayed Africans as childlike, simple, violent, and savage. To correct these stereotypes, Morgan and King emphasize the characteristics that connected Africans to people anywhere in the world. They describe Africans as proud, hardworking, and independent. They write of African farmers as diligent workers who "get up early to go to the fields," help one another through a system of "cooperative work," and "work very hard for a living," defending their produce from rainy seasons, birds, and insects.[27] Countering negative stereotypes of African intelligence, Morgan and King also praise African inventive genius, especially their early mastery of ironwork. From designing housing compounds built with slanted roofs that drained stormwater, to practicing crop rotation to make sure that soil was never exhausted, to creating intricate weavings and pottery for commercial and ceremonial purposes, Africans are shown as intelligent and resourceful, far from the savages, brutes, and heathens of American popular imagination.

By dispelling the myth that Africa was a "bastion of primitiveness," Morgan and King work to present a more accurate and complete picture of the continent and its history.[28] The subsequent sections of their curriculum expand this historical revision to African-descended peoples in the New World.

"Always Looking Westward": Black Explorers and Adventurers

Confronting myths about Africa and its peoples was only the first piece of the historical narrative that Morgan and King constructed. Next came a reappraisal of the contributions of people of African descent in the New World. The standard sixth-grade course of study for Chicago's students included a unit titled "How the Spirit of Exploration Carries On," which told the stories of European explorers from the sixteenth century onward. Morgan and King pair this unit with their own section "Negroes in Discovery and Exploration," which brings to light the stories of Black people who participated in these expeditions. The presentation of famous explorers was already a familiar subject in Black-authored textbooks, where the characters were positioned as companions or aides to more well-known Europeans, offering a counterimage to the depictions of Africans as enslaved only. As with the descriptions of Africa, King and Morgan use the section on exploration to elevate Black agency and accomplishment.[29]

The section on Black explorers begins with Alonzo Pietro, a figure of North African descent who piloted one of Christopher Columbus's ships during his initial voyage to the Caribbean in 1492. Morgan and King credit Pietro, the "Black captain," with saving the expedition and Columbus himself by refusing to leave when other crew memebers grew "tired," "weary," and "impatient," abandoning him in the West

Indies. The authors contrast the actions of the other crew members with those of Pietro, who proved steadfast throughout the dangerous voyage and returned Columbus safely to Spain.[30] The theme of Africans as capable members of exploratory expeditions continues through the stories of Nuflo de Olano, who along with the Spanish explorer Balboa explored the Pacific Ocean and what is now Panama, and the Black men who served with Cortez in his conquest of Mexico.

While Pietro and others are mentioned in the *Supplementary Units*, Estevancio, also called Estevan or Esteban, an enslaved North African who was part of the ill-fated expedition of Pánfilo de Narváez in 1528, receives a majority of Morgan and King's attention. Blown off course and shipwrecked en route to Mexico from Cuba, Estevancio eventually landed in Florida. He and other survivors undertook an arduous journey that lasted several years before finally making their way into Mexico. Once back in Spanish territory, Morgan and King relate to readers, Estevancio became attached to another expedition, this time to locate the fabled cities of Cibola. Because of his facility with Indigenous languages, he scouted for the expedition, riding days ahead of the main party, and became the first non-Indigenous person to arrive in the lands that now make up the states of New Mexico and Arizona.

In Morgan and King's work Estevancio is painted as a heroic figure due to his adaptability in the face of trying conditions and his facility in learning Indigenous languages and cultures. This treatment was in line with other Black textbook authors of the period. Benjamin Brawley called his story "the best authenticated case of a Negro's leading in exploration."[31] Woodson praised him even among other Black explorers as "one who wrote his name still higher in the hall of fame."[32] Eppse eulogized him and the other survivors of Narváez's group as "the first pathfinders across the North American continent," noting that they traveled "over four thousand miles, crossing desert plains, and climbing rugged mountains, and following deep canyons—always looking westward."[33] He also compared Estevancio's journey across the American Southwest to that of the Lewis and Clark expedition nearly three centuries later, noting that he saw "the Mississippi and the buffalo long before the French and the English explorer." For Black textbook writers, Estevancio's survival and his early presence in the American West clearly marked him as a unique figure.

Unlike Woodson, Eppse, or Brawley, Morgan and King choose to end their unit on exploration with a more contemporary story, that of Matthew Henson. By the time the teachers wrote the *Supplementary Units*, Henson's 1908 expedition to the North Pole as part of Admiral Robert Peary's mission had largely faded from public remembrance. Henson himself had fallen from fame and been "forced to take a porter's job at 16 dollars a week," a fate that *Crisis* writer J. A. Roger doubted would have awaited a white explorer and naturalist of his stature.[34] However, Henson was not forgotten within the Black community, and Morgan and King resuscitated the explorer's former glory in their short biographic entry. Drawing from Henson's own 1912 account of his life and adventures, the authors emphasize the fact that by the time he began to work for Peary, Henson was already an experienced traveler, having left school at fourteen to go to sea as a cabin boy aboard merchant vessels, which granted him the opportunity to travel widely to "China, Japan, the Philippines, Africa, France, and Russia."[35] They also highlight Henson's character, presenting him as an ambitious and studious figure who "would always do the things he was told to do and a little more" and would "always read to find out more about the tasks assigned to him." Thus Henson, who could build igloos and speak with native Eskimos in their own languages, drive dog sleds "better than any man living," and repair broken equipment in freezing conditions, emerges as an equal in every way to Peary in the *Supplementary Units*, a fearless and intelligent explorer able to brave treacherous conditions and at last plant the flag of the United States at the very top of the world.[36]

At a time when white historians insisted that Black people took no part in the early history of the US, the *Supplementary Units* carved out important argumentative and discursive space. They showed that African Americans were not only present but that, importantly for

Morgan and King's young audience, they were "as full of adventure as the men with whom they travelled"—in other words, equal in bravery and fortitude to their white counterparts.[37] The acknowledgment of Black participation in these historical moments was significant, and Morgan and King insist on foregrounding such material in their work. However, the approach was not without its limitations. By elevating Africans who were sometimes enslaved to the status of equal partners in exploration, they paper over questions of how much agency these figures could really claim. Additionally, the material does not offer any challenge to the project of colonization itself, instead placing Africans and African Americans in the same position as white European conquerors. The units fell in line with the sentiment expressed in the NAACP's *Crisis* that "the explorer, whether his motive was plunder, the spread of the gospel, knowledge, or romance, has been the pioneer, the sole pioneer, of civilization."[38]

"As Harsh as Truth, and as Uncompromising as Justice":
Slavery, Abolition, and the Civil War
Next, Morgan and King turned to American history, specifically slavery and the Civil War, topics that were often distorted in white-authored texts. Though the North had won the armed conflict, by the early twentieth century it was clear that the South had triumphed in the battle over how the struggle would be portrayed and remembered. Political pressure exerted by groups such as the United Confederate Veterans and the United Daughters of the Confederacy pushed writers and publishers, in both the North and South, to create textbooks that adopted "Lost Cause narratives" in order to avoid controversy and "appease Southern readers."[39] The result of this "devil's bargain" was that school histories disregarded or excused the inherent brutality and horror of the slave system, romanticized plantation life, and painted the fall of the southern slaveholding regime as the defeat of a noble if ultimately doomed cause.[40]

As W. E. B. Du Bois wrote, these efforts amounted to much more than "mere omission and difference of emphasis" and instead constituted an "attempt so to change the facts of history that the story will make pleasant reading for Americans." The result was history so distorted and diluted that "in the end nobody seems to have done anything wrong and everybody was right." Through the *Supplementary Units*, Morgan and King challenge this established narrative.[41]

Morgan and King begin their sections on American slavery, covered in the fifth- and seventh-grade materials, by describing the violence of the slave trade and Middle Passage through which enslaved Africans were transported to the New World. This was significant because, as Lawrence Reddick observed, the majority of history texts offered only "scant reference to the 'trip over.'"[42] In comparison, the *Supplementary Units* describe the capture of Africans through intertribal war and kidnapping expeditions in which the weak or defenseless were stolen from their homes. "Kidnapping raids were often made on villages while the men were away at war and many of the victims of such raids were young people. Slave hunting expeditions became the common method."[43]

Similarly, Morgan and King do not shy away from describing the conditions that enslaved men, women, and children were forced to endure as they made their way from the West African coast to the Caribbean and North America. Their description of the Middle Passage attests to the horrifying nature of the journey: "The slaves were put in chains, which prevented them from escaping or causing trouble. Because of the crowded, stuffy ships many of the slaves died before the end of the journey. Contagious diseases often broke out. Smallpox was one of the common and dreaded diseases. A captain counted on losing one-fourth of his cargo and frequently he lost many more." Their unsparing depiction of abhorrent conditions counteracts the assumption that the slave trade was somehow a humane endeavor. Morgan and King also describe resistance, noting that Africans often took part in uprisings and were "likely to take revenge at any moment." The picture of Africans as submissive or docile was thus replaced with men and women who fought and often died in the attempt to reclaim their freedom. As Morgan and King emphasize, African captives "were not satisfied as slaves. They wanted to live and work as free men."[44]

Another popularly accepted element of American history that Morgan and King contend with is the romanticizing of slavery and southern antebellum life. White-authored accounts of slavery in US history texts showed a paternalistic and benevolent institution, in which enslaved people were childlike dependents cared for by planters who exercised strict but ultimately necessary control.[45] Writers emphasized the idea that Africans' innate inferiority made them unfit and unable to shoulder the burdens of freedom. For example, Mabel B. Casner and Ralph Henry Gabriel's *Exploring American History* described the average enslaved person as "ignorant and careless," unable to complete even rudimentary tasks and liable to break tools and damage costly materials without the guiding hand of the "wise planter" for whom he toiled.[46] In these accounts, slavery was presented not only as a necessary system but as one in which the enslaved contributed little while gaining much. A description of slavery in the mid-Atlantic in *America's Roots in the Past* by Daniel J. Beeby exemplifies this type of narrative:

> On the tobacco plantations of Maryland, Virginia, and North Carolina, the slaves were usually treated kindly. The climate was healthful, and the labor of growing tobacco was easy. The work was so simple that it was well suited to unskilled workers. Even when an overseer was employed to direct the slaves, the work was more or less under the master's observation, as he usually lived on his plantation the year round. In winter the slaves' life was easy. Their work consisted of clearing a piece of land, cutting wood for the fireplaces of the master's mansion, and caring for the livestock.[47]

Beeby goes on to explain that the enslaved were provided with "plenty of plain food," chickens and gardens that were "their own property," and living quarters that, while rudimentary, were "probably better than those of the first settlers of Virginia in Plymouth." Overall, then, Beeby presents slavery as a benefit to all involved.[48]

Morgan and King refuse to be complicit in the justification of slavery as a benevolent institution. Instead, they tell students that conditions varied widely and that "some of the masters were harsh and unfeeling; some were kind and humane; others were indifferent." To show this range the authors provide two examples based on primary source accounts, one the Fairdale plantation in Tennessee and the other the plantation of Colonel Lloyd in Maryland, where Frederick Douglass was born and spent his early childhood. On the Fairdale plantation, the better of the two, the enslaved people were allowed to tend small gardens of their own after their day's work, furnished with new clothing and shoes twice a year, regularly visited by physicians, and spared the use of whipping in most instances. This description, although not nearly as saccharine as white textbooks of the period, which emphasized the paternalism of planters and the grateful loyalty of those who were enslaved, includes many of the elements that white authors relied on to argue the benefits of the slave system.[49]

If Morgan and King had ended their discussion of plantation life with Fairdale, they would have closely approximated the standard narrative of slavery as presented by white authors. However, they use the plantation of Colonel Lloyd to offer a sharp counterpoint. At Lloyd's plantation, the reader is told, the enslaved lived in "low rough buildings" and "scattered huts," which were "filled to overflowing with slave families." As a result, they were "dirty and ill kept." Food consisted of "pickled pork" and "Indian meal" and very little of even this. Work began at daybreak and lasted unabated until it was "too dark to see." Morgan and King not only describe these conditions but also show the violence that underlay them: "Whipping was the order of the day, and no one, woman or child, old or young, was safe from it." In white-authored history textbooks, physical punishment was described as little used or justified as a fitting end for the disobedient or lazy, yet Morgan and King depict this brutality as a fundamental and indiscriminate part of slavery itself.[50]

Morgan and King also use their descriptions of slavery to defend the skill and value of Black labor. In the fifth-grade section on plantation life, Morgan and King describe the duties of planters, overseers, and enslaved people. Instead of the standard descriptions of the slaved as lazy, childlike, or inept, the authors instead emphasize their skill and ability. They remark that enslaved men and women not only worked in the fields but were also skilled "carpenters, masons, wheelwrights, coopers, blacksmiths, sailors, typesetters, miners, engineers, mechanics, jewelers, and silversmiths." They add, "Some slave mechanics could not only build but also draw plans, make contracts, and complete a house."[51] Not only were the enslaved often skilled craftsmen, Morgan and King insist, they were also inventors. When the *Supplementary Units* cover the cotton gin, for instance, the authors reveal that it was enslaved Africans who pioneered much of the technology, having "experimented with certain appliances for the separation of the seed from the cotton" long before Eli Whitney drew on these existing designs to patent his own device.[52] By describing the range of occupations performed by the enslaved, many of which required skill and specialized knowledge, Morgan and King dignify the physical and mental work of the enslaved and undercut arguments that their work was confined to simple or unimportant tasks.

Along with honoring the sacrifices made by those who remained enslaved, Morgan and King also highlight the bravery of the men and women who risked their lives to resist the slave system, whether runaways, rebels, free Black people, or abolitionists. The *Supplementary Units* celebrate the agency of those who managed to "steal away" to freedom. As Morgan and King tell their audience, "a very large number of slaves *freed themselves* [emphasis mine] by running away to the northern states and Canada."[53] The *Supplementary Units* emphasize the presence of persons who, whether through manumission, self-purchase, or escape, became free before the Civil War, a subject that received scant attention in standard history texts. However, even though these men and women were no longer held in bondage, the authors pointed out that they were often only "half free" because of restrictions that kept them from voting, holding public office, or participating in local militias.

Morgan and King emphasize that this did not stop many free Black people from attaining some measure of financial and social independence. The *Supplementary Units* relate the stories of prominent businessmen like Joseph C. Casey and William Platt of western New York who both became involved in lumber mills, inventors like Henry Blair of Maryland who patented a corn harvester, and industrialists like Robert Gordon of Virginia who became wealthy through managing several successful coal-mining operations. Morgan and King use the stories of these prosperous free men to complicate the assumption that all Black people had occupied subservient positions in antebellum society.[54]

Abolitionists and their role in the nation's past also received a new appraisal in Morgan and King's curriculum. In white-authored texts these figures had been depicted as wild-eyed fanatics who hindered the supposed good-faith efforts of both the North and the South and pushed the nation toward war. For example, Casner and Gabriel portrayed William Lloyd Garrison, the antislavery leader whose newspaper *The Liberator* acted as a mouthpiece for the movement, as an unreasoned agitator who "paid no attention to the fact that slavery had been handed down from colonial times and that no man living in the United States in his day was responsible for it." They went on to blame "the bitterness and unfairness" of Garrison and other abolitionists as a major force that pushed the nation into war.[55] Thus responsibility for the conflict is shifted away from the morally abhorrent nature of chattel slavery and the individuals and institutions that supported it and instead placed on a small group of antislavery advocates, whom the authors shun as extremists for abandoning the path of compromise and gradualism. As scholar Leah Washburn points out, these depictions emphasize "the dangers of political radicalism" instead of the injustice of human bondage itself.[56]

The Garrison that appears in the *Supplementary Units* is a different figure than the extremist of white-authored histories. Instead, he is a heroic figure who dared to speak truth to power and denounce slavery as a "moral evil."[57] Morgan and King quote a passage from *The Liberator*, "a stirring document against slavery and slaveholders," in order to impress the nature of Garrison's resolve upon their readers: "I will be as harsh as truth and as uncompromising as justice. . . . Urge me not to use moderation in a cause like the present. I am in earnest—I will not equivocate—I will not excuse—I will not retreat a single inch—and I will be heard." The passage captures in dramatic fashion the bold and uncompromising nature of Garrison and other abolitionists and cast them as "brave people" who fought "for the cause of freedom." Where white-authored textbooks saw someone to be shunned, Morgan and King saw figure students might emulate in his conviction to hold the nation to account.[58]

While Morgan and King give coverage to white abolitionists like Garrison for their influential role in defying the slave system, they are also careful to point out that it was Black people themselves who initiated and sustained the abolitionist movement. This is a key point, since, as Black educator Lawrence Reddick commented in the 1930s, most textbooks depicted abolitionism as a northern white phenomenon in which Black people "did nothing, or at the very most, very little, toward their own freedom."[59] In contrast, the majority of the abolitionists covered in the *Supplementary Units*, seven out of nine names mentioned, are Black leaders. Names that have now become, but were not at the time, standard textbook material—such as Frederick Douglass the famed orator and author of the antislavery paper *The North Star*; Harriet Tubman, the underground railroad conductor and Union spy whom readers were told braved "dark swamps, going hungry, and unrelenting cold and fear" on multiple missions to free her people; and Sojourner Truth, the activist and leader who was critical to President Abraham Lincoln's decision to allow Black troops to fight in the Civil War—are each covered in turn. Even more impressively, lesser-known figures like abolitionist Josiah Henson, antislavery organizer William Stell, and lecturer Charles L. Redmond also receive praise. Overall, the abolitionist movement is framed in terms of Black people seeking their own liberation.[60]

This focus on Black agency continues in Morgan and King's appraisal of the Civil War, which emphasizes the active participation of both free and enslaved Black people in preserving the Union and putting an end to the slave system. The authors identify slavery and its extension as the direct cause of the Civil War. Whereas white-authored textbooks tended to obscure the causes of the conflict in vague arguments about states' rights, Morgan and King observe that the underlying issue was the South's ability to maintain political power in order to "protect itself from attacks on the slave system" and that the war was "the inevitable end of the bitterness which existed between the states favoring slavery and those opposed to it."[61] These statements echoed Du Bois's conclusion that "of all historic facts there can be none clearer than that for four long and fearful years the South fought to perpetuate human slavery."[62]

Morgan and King also discuss the heroic actions of Black men and women during the war. As they state, "The story of the battles of the Civil War is a familiar one. Less familiar however is the story of the Negro in the War." In the *Supplementary Units*, readers learn that Black people were involved in the war effort from the onset. Morgan and King relate that in the South, slaveholders used coerced Black labor to erect "bridges, roads, and fortifications" in addition to forcing them to serve in Confederate armies. The authors stress that in the North, when given the opportunity, free African Americans were more than ready to take up arms as Union soldiers, as some 186,000 enlisted during the course of the war. The exploits of Black soldiers are highlighted throughout, including the actions of the Fifty-Fourth Massachusetts, the most famous Black regiment organized during the war. Other regiments like those who served in the Army of the Potomac and the Black troops who captured the Confederate batteries at Port Hudson, Louisiana, are also covered. Citing this evidence, Morgan and King conclude that Black Americans "rendered gallant service" to the nation during its greatest crisis.[63] They would return to the theme of Black military service in their coverage of Black Americans in the present.

"Unusual Progress": Reconstruction and Beyond

Reconstruction was perhaps the most deeply mischaracterized period of America's past in the textbooks of the early and mid-1900s. The years immediately following the end of the Civil War were portrayed as a period of misrule where white southerners were forced to endure indignity and victimization at the hands of "ignorant" formerly enslaved people and northern "rascals" who descended on the wounded South.[64] Ruth and Willis M. West's history exemplified this familiar narrative, depicting southern whites as helpless in the face of "disorders from the lawless bands of ex-slaves roaming about their homes" and "the corruption of the carpetbag government."[65] The supposedly wanton cruelty of northerners and freed people toward the vanquished Confederacy was used to justify the imposition of Black codes and Jim Crow legistlation the systematic stripping of Black rights, as defensive measures meant to maintain control of "the shiftless and sometimes vicious freedmen."[66] Even the terrorist campaigns of the Ku Klux Klan were championed as necessary to the preservation of southern society. Casner and Gabriel depicted the Klan as a brave gathering of southern white men who organized to "fight the evils that surrounded them" and "frightened the Negroes and warned the carpetbaggers."[67] Similarly, West and West describe the Klan as a "secret society" whose members, "dressing like ghosts in masks and long white robes . . . rode about at night warning the terrified Negroes to behave themselves and let government affairs alone."[68] For Black students in the classrooms of Migration-era Chicago, many of whom would have had direct knowledge of the Klan, either personally or through family members and intimates, reading these depictions must have added to the trauma and violence they had already experienced.

If Reconstruction was a low point in representation of Black Americans in white-authored history texts, it was also the last mention they received, as Black people were often absent from any discussion of modern political, social, and economic life in the US. West and West's chapter "America Faces New Tasks," for example, covers contemporary issues such as the scientific development of new travel and transportation technologies, social movements such as women's suffrage and child welfare campaigns, and national and global events like the First World War and Great Depression. The writers, however, make no mention of African Americans as individuals or as a social group in any of this material. The impression is that once free, Black people simply faded into the background of the American story, contributing little if anything to the modern world.

When discussing the period from Reconstruction to the present, Morgan and King offer a wholly different account. In the section of the *Supplementary Units* titled "Rebuilding the Nation," they agree with other historians that Reconstruction was a tumultuous period, but they argue that Black Americans, far from idly subsisting on the supposed spoils of war, in actuality suffered more dislocation and derision than any other group. The authors point out that the Emancipation Proclamation provided little beyond an end to legalized bondage and that many of those who were formerly enslaved were left at the end of the war "without homes and without means of support."[69] These obstacles were only overcome by the diligence and faith of the freedmen. Refuting the characterization of Black people as unambitious or idle, Morgan and King present evidence that some 247,333 of them attended schools under the Freedmen's Bureau in order to gain education. They conclude, "It did not take many years for the newly freed Negroes to show the results of education. By 1870, illiteracy of the colored people had been reduced considerably. Many people showed unusual progress."[70]

To illustrate this progress, Morgan and King include several short biographies of prominent Black Americans from the fields of education, invention, science, business, government, history, music, art, and literature. The authors choose a mix of male and female subjects, and as with other sections they include both famous and lesser-known figures ranging from educator Mary McLeod Bethune to politician Blanche K. Bruce to inventor Jan E. Matzeliger. This strategy of highlighting the accomplishments of notable Black people, especially in fields where they otherwise would not have been expected, appears in the work of numerous Black authors. Brawley's *Short History of the American Negro*, for example, contains the chapter "Negro Achievement in

Literature, Art, and Invention"; Eppse and Foster's *An Elementary History of America* provides readers with a chapter on "The Negro's Contribution to American Progress"; and Woodson's *Negro Makers of History* includes two chapters, "Evidences of Progress" and "Higher Strivings," meant to invalidate the claim that "the race stood still after its emancipation."[71] More than a list of accomplishments, these chapters were a tool to rectify exclusion and fundamentally "challenge the dominant constructions of African American mental and intellectual capacity."[72] By highlighting the presence of Black men and women in fields such as law, education, and medicine, they provided evidence against the presumption that Black people were innately or biologically inferior.

Inhabitants of Chicago: Local History and the Culture of Black Chicago

Although Morgan and King in many respects followed the broad outlines of the emerging Black history movement, they also added to this work in ways that were unique and highly localized. The city of Chicago and the neighborhood of Bronzeville emerge throughout the units as characters in their own right. This local approach was popular with progressive pedagogues who insisted on rooting learning in the familiar before venturing out into community, city, and country in successive steps. Morgan and King adapted this approach, focusing on Chicago's Black community and its history, and making a claim for the integral part that Black people would continue to play in the city's future.

This geographic and imaginative reorientation began in the materials for the early grades with a section titled "Some Workers We Meet."[73] Included in these brief few pages were descriptions of Black policemen and Pullman porters, among other local figures. In the eighth-grade units these biographies were revisited and elaborated on in a section called "Achievements of the Negro in Chicago."[74] The list of names is expanded to include prominent historical figures like Jean Baptiste Point du Sable, the first non-Indigenous person to settle in what would become Chicago, and Dr. Daniel Hale Williams, the nineteenth-century physician who was first in the nation to perform open-heart surgery. However, Morgan and King were even more concerned with contemporary achievements like those of chemist Percy Julian, principals Ruth Jackson and Maudelle Bousfield, Judge Albert B. George, and Professor Allison Davis.

Not only were Morgan and King concerned with the biographies of leading Black Chicagoans past and present; they also shone a light on the central institutions of the Black metropolis. The units for second-grade students, which consisted of short stories and poems, were purposefully set in a local context, the George Cleveland Hall Branch Library, where Morgan and King completed much of their initial research. The authors describe the library in warm and inviting language as "a pretty, gray, stone building" where the children's librarian, a woman with a "smiling brown face" and a "low soft voice," almost certainly librarian Charlemae Rollins, enjoys story hours with her young friends. By setting the story within the walls of the Hall Branch, Morgan and King brought an important Black institutional space into their curriculum.[75]

The Hall Branch was not the only institutional fixture of Bronzeville to receive attention, however. In the eighth-grade units, Morgan and King ended with "Suggested Places to Visit," which included the offices of the nationally circulated Black newspaper the *Chicago Defender*, the South Side Community Arts Center, and the newly constructed Ida B. Wells Homes. For Black students, many of these spaces would have been familiar parts of their day-to-day experience. Their inclusion in the *Supplementary Units* established a connection between the wider worlds of history and social studies and the more intimate space of the community they already occupied. For white students, on the other hand, the segregated nature of the city precluded any real knowledge of these people and places. As we will see in chapter 5, reading descriptions of one's "Colored Neighbors" or "Places to Visit" stimulated some white students to ask new questions about parts of their world that, until then, lay outside of their view.[76]

"It Is Not Very Often That Stories Are Written About Colored Soldiers": Military Service Past and Present

Morgan and King's use of local history also played a role in their coverage of African Americans in military life. Historically, military service has been linked to ideas of civic virtue, with the "citizen soldier" seen as a "primary actor in protecting democratic values and individual liberties."[77] Although African Americans possessed a long record of military service, their efforts were often questioned, maligned, and ignored as a way of signaling that Black people themselves, no matter their sacrifice, remained outside full inclusion in American society. As Morgan and King state, "It is not very often that stories are written about colored soldiers."[78] Black historians felt a driving need to preserve and spread knowledge of Black military valor, not only to fill the void in the historical record but also to dismantle the system of racial caste that kept Black people outside of the mainstream of American life. The recognition of their service in the *Supplementary Units* rendered the actions of Black soldiers visible to a larger audience both within and outside of the Black community, beginning with Chicago and the Eighth Illinois National Guard Regiment.

The Eighth saw action during the First World War in the Argonne Forest of France and participated in the Allied advances that finally broke the defenses of the army and led to the conclusion of the war. Several members of the company received commendations for their service, including Sgt. Matthew Jenkins, Lt. William Warfield, and Capt. James H. Smith, each of who was were given the French Cross of War for their bravery on the battlefield.[79] These exploits made the Eighth local heroes, and their headquarters on Giles Street in Chicago was a central piece of community history.

Morgan and King's coverage of Black military service not only provided an opportunity to burnish Black pride but also served as an indictment of the mistreatment of Black veterans during and after the war. Many of the men of the Eighth Infantry, for example, were called on to defend themselves again soon after their return from Europe, this time not against foreign adversaries but against the domestic terror embodied in the race riots of 1919. The hypocrisy of a nation that enlisted Black soldiers but failed to honor or protect them after their service ended was as obvious as it was disturbing. This is a point explicitly addressed by Woodson, who wrote, "The Negro had helped save democracy abroad, but he must fight to enjoy it at home."[80]

"The Negro and Social Justice"

Throughout the *Supplementary Units* Morgan and King focus on presenting material that elevates and enumerates Black achievements in order to make an unimpeachable argument for the importance of Black history to the larger history of the nation. As this chapter makes clear, these were ambitious aims, far beyond what many in Chicago and elsewhere had even attempted. However, the *Supplementary Units* were also conservative by some measures. While they traced the oppression inherent in American slavery, for example, Morgan and King did not directly address the disenfranchisement and disillusionment faced by many contemporary Black Americans as a result of the racist legal and social structures under which they lived.

In some ways Morgan and King's choice to center their materials on positive narratives instead of systemic critiques was reflective of the kinds of history produced by Black scholars during the early twentieth century more generally. Because Black history had yet to gain the recognition it would enjoy in the 1960s and beyond, most Black historians, including those who wrote for younger audiences, were concerned with moving Black stories from "the margins to the mainstream." As a result, their works were "often preoccupied with integrating African American history into mainstream U.S. History," which they considered a necessary first step toward both Black advancement and prejudice reduction among whites.[81]

This is not to say that early Black historians avoided critique of present-day racism altogether. Benjamin Brawley's textbook *A Short History of the American Negro*, although containing much of the achievement-centered narrative found in the *Supplementary Units*, commented pointedly on the political and economic disenfranchisement of Black Americans in the post-Reconstruction era, stating that "separate and inferior traveling accommodations, especially meager provision for the education of Negro children, inadequate street, lighting, and water facilities in most cities and towns, and the general lack of protection of life and property" each "made life all the harder for the Negro people."[82] Woodson's *The Negro in Our History* was even more incisive. In his last chapter, titled "The Negro and Social Justice," Woodson spoke directly to the issues of racism and segregation, including the "disturbing prejudice" seen in northern cities following increased Black migration, the lack of equal economic opportunity for Black Americans, and the ever-present "problem of earning a living." He even railed against the "so-called statistics" created by biased researchers and institutions who claimed to study race but instead "devised various schemes to make a case for the natural superiority of the white man." Morgan and King drew extensively from both Woodson and Brawley, among others, but they tended to take the most positive aspects instead of these more condemning elements.[83]

There are two likely reasons for the absence of more openly critical material in the *Supplementary Units*. The first is the context in which they were produced. Brawley and Woodson were part of institutions, Morehouse College and the Association for the Study of Negro Life and History, respectively, which offered relatively safe spaces from which to launch more critical assaults on racism. Morgan and King, working within the white-controlled Chicago Public Schools on a project that was experimental and thus tenuous, may have felt they had far less latitude. Additionally, the wartime demand for patriotic material and the thoroughgoing dedication of CPS to the doctrine of "Americanism" meant that any curriculum that openly challenged the outlines of American exceptionalism would stand little chance of approval. Morgan and King had gained a foothold for Black voices within the city's curriculum, but as historian Jonathan Zimmerman has noted, the price paid by ethnic and racialized minorities for inclusion in US history has often been a willingness to embrace a "triumphal narrative" that deemphasizes the nation's faults.[84]

In addition to their possible reluctance to engage in topics that may have led to censorship, there is also evidence to suggest that Morgan and King believed that an approach concentrating on the positive aspects of the Black past would prove effective in reducing prejudice and reinforcing the recognition of Black citizenship. Morgan held the view of many progressive educators, white and Black, that at its root racial antipathy was a matter of ignorance and "incomplete views."[85] If students were given a chance to learn that peoples of all backgrounds had played a part in the drama of American history, Morgan argued, prejudice would lessen and the groundwork would be laid for social and political progress. As Morgan stated, "It is my firm belief that this educational method . . . will bring about a change in the kind and quality of attitude in our American family and gradually bring about a change in interracial as well as racial behavior." Whether Morgan's faith in education as a tool of social change would be rewarded would only be seen as the *Supplementary Units* made their way into communities and classrooms.

"The Negro Has Made and Is Still Making His Contribution": *Assessing the* Supplementary Units

Analysis of the content of the *Supplementary Units* reveals that they were without question part of the broader tradition of the alternative Black curriculum. The two authors refuted stereotypes and racist caricatures and presented a new discourse around Black identity based on themes such as the importance of African civilization and its diasporic connection to the New World; depictions of slavery, the Civil War, and Reconstruction that highlighted Black agency and resistance; and descriptions of Black Americans' historical contributions to the nation as soldiers, statesmen, inventors, intellectuals, and cultural icons. These elements were brought to bear in a deliberate and well-organized manner to challenge and fundamentally "alter the racial meanings associated with Blackness."[86] They showed beyond a shadow of doubt that, as Morgan and King stated, "The Negro has made and is still making his contribution to American life." The responses to the units, from educators and academics, parents and students, soldiers and civilians, would soon determine how much this vision resonated.

A coffee hour,
To talk and sip
And pin a flower
Or pass a glance
At Soror Morgan
Who is our guest
And quite the pride
Of the Middle West
Come friends—Like bees,
To Douglass swarm,
Our honor is
An "Old School Marm"
Now if with us
You'll share this fun
Dial w-o
0–2–3–1

—Poem for a Phi Delta
Kappa Event in Morgan's
Honor at Douglass
Community House in
Chicago, Soror Johnson,
February 12, 1944[1]

CHAPTER 4

"AND QUITE THE PRIDE OF THE MIDDLE WEST"

The *Supplementary Units*, Influence
and Impact, 1942–1945

$\mathcal{J}$UNE 12, 1942—A little over a month after the adoption of the
Supplementary Units into the curriculum of Chicago's public schools,
some three hundred people gathered at the Women's City Club in Chicago for a celebratory dinner. The attendees, educators, activists, and
political, social, and religious leaders met to show their enthusiasm for
the "revolutionary trend" that promised to "integrate the Negro into
the regulation course of history taught in all Chicago public schools,
from the first to the eighth grades." The banquet, held by the women
of the Phi Delta Kappa sorority, included several of the major luminaries of the city's Black community. Seated at the table of honor
alongside Superintendent Johnson, Madeline Morgan, and her collab-
orator and research assistant Bessie Smith were prominent attorney
and political figure Earl Dickerson, Urban League president Frayser
Lane, and NAACP representative Oscar Brown. Also at the table were
Wendell Phillips High School history teacher Samuel Stratton, Willard M. Payne representing the Negro Chamber of Commerce, and
the Rev. Sam Gandy.[1]

These men, however, were eclipsed and outnumbered by educators like Ruth Jackson, the principal of Colman Elementary, and Annabel Prescott, the dean of girls for Wendell Phillips High School. Also in attendance was Oneida Cockrell, the former supreme basileus (national leader) of Phi Delta Kappa, and Maudelle Bousfield, the pioneering principal, who along with the dozens of other assorted educators and sorors represented the strength and interconnectedness of the networks of Black women who had supported Morgan from the beginning.[2] These women came to the celebration out of a sense of pride, solidarity, and sisterhood. Although the dinner was formally meant to recognize Superintendent Johnson, who received praise for his forward thinking on matters of race, the *Chicago Defender* echoed what many already knew when it revealed that "the original idea for the departure in teaching history in Chicago schools was broached by Mrs. Madeline Morgan."[3] It was also Morgan, along with Bessie King, not Johnson or the board of education, who had written and tested the curriculum and "chiefly conducted the research work." Johnson may have been the honored guest that night, but there was no doubt that Morgan was the star.

"There Is No Reason Why Every School System in the United States . . . Should Not Adopt This Program": The Supplementary Units and Black Educators

The banquet that summer would not be the last time Morgan and her work drew attention and applause. Between 1942 and 1945, the *Supplementary Units* would be embraced and endorsed by a dizzying number of publications and persons. In the Black community, the curriculum was recognized as an extension of the growing Black history movement and its broader goals of equality and full inclusion in American society. In the white community, on the other hand, it was primarily seen as a means of easing the racial tensions boiling over in American cities and classrooms, especially in the aftermath of the riots that consumed the summer of 1943. Calls for Morgan's work, and for her presence as an expert in the field of intercultural education, would come from various school districts, communities, civil rights groups, and religious organizations, and the modest sixth-grade social studies teacher would find herself an unlikely celebrity in both academic circles and the popular press. At the same time, even as she gained the stature as a noted voice on intercultural relations and Black history, Morgan was also often depicted in ways that downplayed elements of her accomplishments to make them more palatable for white, and sometimes Black, audiences. Tracing the ways Morgan shows up in spaces marked for different groups—readers of academic journals and casual observers of the popular press, Black audiences and white ones, scholars and classroom teachers—gives us a better understanding of how Black women were represented in each.

Much of the recognition Morgan received during this period would begin with or flow through the Association for the Study of Negro Life and History (ASNLH), the organization that served as her primary base for intellectual development and social activism. When the association met for its twenty-eighth annual conference, held October 29–31, 1943, in Detroit, Morgan was on hand. That Saturday, October 30, at 10:00 a.m., she participated in a session titled "How We Study the Negro."[4] True to the diverse makeup of the ASNLH membership, the panel was presided over by a high school principal, Charles A. Daly, and included both a university-level academic, Mrs. Constance Ridley Heslip, instructor in race relations at the University of Toledo, and a secondary teacher, Herman Dreer of the St. Louis Public Schools, as presenters alongside Morgan, who was herself a teacher in the primary grades. Morgan's presentation, "The Study of the Negro in the Chicago Public Schools," centered on her role as co-author of the *Supplementary Units*, and was well received and remarked on as "a convincing account of what is now being done systematically in Chicago to give the Negro the same place in the curriculum as that provided for the study of the Greek, the Latin and the Teuton." Morgan's advocating for Black history within Chicago's schools must have struck her listeners as particularly impressive, because the next morning, during the general session, Morgan's work again came up for comment, most likely pushed to the fore by sorors from Detroit's local

Chi chapter of Phi Delta Kappa. The association "unanimously voted to invite the attention of other school systems to the commendable step made in the study of the Negro in Chicago under the stimulus of Mrs. Madeline R. Morgan and to urge upon educational authorities elsewhere to emulate this example."[5] At a conference which that year included addresses and presentations from overwhelmingly male luminaries such as Woodson protégé Lorenzo Johnston Greene, Charles H. Wesley, Horace Mann Bond, and John Hope Franklin, Morgan had managed not only to be heard but also to gain a significant amount of praise from others involved in the work of producing and popularizing Black history.

Word of the strong impression made by Morgan at the Detroit conference traveled quickly. In December 1943, Phi Delta Kappa's supreme basileus, Gertrude Robinson, wrote that although she had not been able to attend the association meeting in person, she was enthusiastic about Morgan's success and glad that "Chi offered a resolution, which the association gladly adopted."[6] She then moved on to the main purpose of her message, the NAACP's Spingarn Medal. The award, created in 1914 by Jewish academic and NAACP board chairman Joel Elias Spingarn, was given each year to mark "the highest or noblest achievement by an American Negro during the preceding year," whether "intellectual, spiritual, physical, scientific, commercial, educational or any other."[7] In the medal's twenty-nine-year hisotry history it had been given to a woman only three times, to suffragist and civil rights leader Mary Burnett Talbert, educator and activist Mary McLeod Bethune, and opera singer Marian Anderson, yet Robinson was convinced that Morgan stood a chance at the prestigious award in 1943 and was busy marshaling an effort to ensure her consideration. As she wrote:

> The plan is as follows: Marion Bluitt is to write a letter to the Chairman of each branch of the NAACP, and include a copy of your accomplishments, and a story about yourself. The Chairmen will be asked to send their vote to the Spingarn Committee, if they feel that your work merits the medal.

This method will give each Chairman the opportunity to study your work and it will give each a clearer idea of what the work is all about. Quotations, comments, resolutions, etc. should all be included in the statement you submit. No doubt you have heard from Marion concerning this. Will you please get this article to her as soon as possible? We are all anxious about it.

Sororally,

Gertrude A. Robinson[8]

Robinson's enthusiasm was palpable, and her strategy paid dividends. Proof that Morgan's Spingarn campaign acquired support is provided by the coverage it received in the influential *Pittsburgh Courier*, which only a few months after Robinson's letter declared, "Our candidate for the 1943 Spingarn Medal is Mrs. Madeline Robinson Morgan, a Chicago school teacher, who has devised, and had accepted by the Chicago school system, a course of study in the elementary schools which will eliminate race prejudice at its very beginning."[9] The *Courier* noted that the information contained in the units on "the contributions and achievements of Negroes, their African background," and "their history and experiences" would do much to counter racism, segregation, and discrimination. As the paper stated, prodding policy makers in New York and across the nation: "There is no reason why every school system in the United States—regardless of section—should not adopt this program. . . . Certainly a democratic country should recognize as quickly as totalitarian countries that the future belongs to the youth, and that if the future is to be what we want it to be, children must be taught early what we want them to know." Despite such support, Morgan did not win the NAACP's most celebrated award. That year's selection was William Hastie, the former dean of Howard Law School who resigned from his position as civilian aide to the US secretary of war in protest over the mistreatment of Black soldiers.[10] However, even without the prestigious medal, Morgan was gaining significant notoriety.

Without the Spingarn, Phi Delta Kappa chose to honor Morgan in another way. On February 19, 1944, Morgan and King attended a luncheon in Washington, DC, at Howard University's Slowe Hall. The location was a fitting one. Named for Lucy Diggs Slowe, the first dean of women at the historic Black college, who served from 1922 until 1937, the hall reflected the legacy of an educator and administrator who had worked to carve out space for Black women to assume leadership in modern society. As president and founder of the first Black women's sorority, Alpha Kappa Alpha, a progressive secondary school teacher and administrator in Baltimore, and the inaugural dean of women at her alma mater of Howard, Slowe had sought to train younger generations of Black women activists who were "liberally educated, socially aware, and capable of putting their talents into action for the common, democratic good."[11] Morgan's campaign to influence Chicago's wartime curriculum, one that entailed demanding to be seen as an expert and leader in the male-dominated spaces of Chicago's educational hierarchy and in the Black history movement itself, embodied much of Slowe's attitude and ambition.

At the ceremony at Slowe Hall, with over 150 educators from throughout the country present, Morgan became the first recipient of a newly created National Sorority of Phi Delta Kappa Achievement Award, given "in recognition and encouragement for meritorious achievement." Robinson was on hand to present Morgan with the prize, and King also received a certificate of honor and ceremonial key. The keynote address was given by Carter G. Woodson, who "stressed the significance of the accomplishments of the honored guests," a continuation of his earlier support of the *Supplementary Units*, which he had championed since Morgan first spoke to him about the possibility of attempting such a project in the late 1930s.[12]

The day after the ceremony in Washington, DC, Morgan and King turned north to New York. Recently, Morgan had been named as one of twelve members of a "Race Relations Honor Roll," the result of a nationwide poll created by the city's Schomburg Center of Negro Literature and its curator, Lawrence D. Reddick, to recognize figures who had "done most during the past year for the improvement of race relations 'in terms of real democracy.'"[13] The list of honorees for 1943 included impressive and well-known figures like actress Lena Horne, intellectual luminary W. E. B. Du Bois, screenwriter Carlton Moss, and dancer Katherine Dunham. That Morgan's name was listed among the honorees reveals just how far her impact had spread.

While in New York, Morgan and King attended the annual Negro History Week breakfast hosted by that city's branch of the ASNLH located at the Grand Street Boys Association at 106 West Fifty-Fifth Street. The event was a large one, with over nine hundred attendees in the hall and many others turned away for lack of room. The *New York Amsterdam News*, a Black daily, wrote excitedly that among the other speakers, "Mrs. Morgan's visit and address fired the imagination, inspired the purpose and steeled the determination of a larger number of persons than ever before who have been brought under the dynamic influence of Negro History as an instrument of democracy, inter-racial understanding, and progress."[14] Using Morgan's success in Chicago as an example, the paper criticized the relative failure of New York, and in particular its Mayor Fiorello LaGuardia, to take similar measures, despite the calls of the teachers' union, the Permanent Committee for Better Schools in Harlem, the City-Wide Citizens' Committee on Harlem, and other organizations. The adoption of Morgan's work had, according to the *News*, "set a swift pace for the proud and sometimes boastful city of New York to follow," as "now, like never before, New York's claim to leadership in inter-racial understanding and democratic ways of life and living stands in second place, with Chicago in front." In its use of Morgan and her work as an example to be emulated even in "boastful" New York, the article pointed to the fact that Morgan's work was taken up to push for similar changes in other cities.

The press coverage through ASNLH and Phi Delta Kappa was not simply personal affirmation or publicity; it served to carry Morgan's work far beyond the urban centers of Chicago and New York. Indeed, as the *Supplementary Units* continued to circulate among Black educators, they found receptive audiences in smaller cities that used her example to improve their own curricular offerings. Russell W. Smith, a Black administrator working in the tiny hamlet of East Moline, Illinois, two hours west of Chicago, wrote to Morgan in October 1943 to request copies of her work and express his resolve to see that the material was incorporated into the curriculum there. As he put it, "I am very interested in securing such a course for the purpose of study and eventual incorporation into the Social Studies material at Campbell School, a six grade, all Negro school of which I am principal. I feel there is a definite need of such a supplementary unit in all schools that all students might be educated to the facts concerning the development of Our Race."[15] Houston R. Jackson, the supervisor of history and civics for the Colored Schools of Baltimore, wrote to Morgan the next month, stating that he had "for several months" followed the news of her "commendable effort in organizing units of work in the field of Negro History." Jackson too asked for copies of the *Supplementary Units* for his own "study and investigation" and "with a view to proposing their adoption in our system."[16]

The next year, the NAACP of East Liverpool, Ohio, formed a committee to push for the inclusion of Black history as part of the required curriculum for their district. Meeting with Superintendent M. W. Essex, the group "gave him particulars of the plan now being used in Chicago schools" and noted that "Mrs. Madeline R. Morgan, had provided the group with an outline of the Chicago system, and a list of approved texts now being used there."[17] The same group then presented to the town's board of education, arguing that Youngstown and Cleveland were already taking up Morgan's curriculum for discussion and possible use. Although the board of education did not fully commit to using Morgan's curriculum at that session, her success was clearly being used by Black educators and activists to pressure local school districts to change curricula.

In the Jim Crow South, Morgan's work was also seen as potentially groundbreaking. In June 1943, Walter E. Morial of the New Orleans Teachers' Association, the union that represented Black teachers in deeply segregated Louisiana, wrote to Morgan with a request for "a copy of the course of study and curriculum that you have worked out" and his wishes for her "continued success in your program."[18] In February 1944, Cohen T. Simpson, the vice president of State Teachers College in Montgomery and chairman of the Program Committee for the yearly meeting of the Alabama State Teachers' Association, wrote to Morgan to invite her as a speaker on the topic of "human relations." As Simpson put it, "We have not done much in our systems on race education." Morgan's example, Simpson believed, would be instructive to the Black teachers of Alabama, and possibly provide a blueprint for building "a program of race pride" even in the "heart of the South." Like Black educators in northern cities like Baltimore and East Liverpool, Ohio, southern Black teachers also understood Morgan's accomplishment as a victory for the race that could be emulated in other settings. The interest and enthusiasm her work stirred made it clear that her ideas were being read, discussed, and debated in school systems large and small throughout the early 1940s.[19]

In an age before modern technology seamlessly connected communities of educators nationwide, Morgan was adept at making the best of the modes of communication open to her, chief among them the world of printed publications. One of the most influential of these was the ASNLH's *Negro History Bulletin* (*NHB*). Staffed and read largely by Black women schoolteachers, librarians, and administrators, the magazine became "an arena in which black women, mainly school teachers and social activists, could articulate their concerns about educating black youth, reforming American society, and uplifting the masses of their people."[20] The pages of the *NHB* allowed Morgan and her work to be acknowledged and utilized by Black educators throughout the country.

Morgan was first introduced to readers of the *NHB* in February 1943. The piece described her trajectory upward through the Chicago Public Schools, first as a student and then as a teacher, emphasizing her "invention," "enterprise," and work toward bringing the school system in line with the principles of "real democracy," including a truer accounting of the nation's history.[21] The effort at building a Negro history curriculum in Chicago was, the journal insisted, a product of her singular drive and determination. Morgan's position as a classroom teacher and pedagogical expert made her uniquely qualified for this work because as the authors put it, "Those who had acceptable methods of presenting such data on the Negro knew little to present and those well informed on the background and current status of the Negro knew practically nothing about imparting these facts according to the latest educational methods." The authors recognized that Morgan's formal education combined with her experience in the classroom allowed her to bridge a divide between what we would now describe as the content knowledge of Black history and the pedagogical knowledge of teaching methods and appropriate strategies to communicate this history to a younger audience.

While the *NHB* piece was largely laudatory of Morgan and her accomplishments, it also included sections that adopted a somewhat patronizing tone in estimating the value of her contributions. For instance, the authors seemed surprised that the work began in a sorority, noting that "the interesting thing is that the idea originated in a sorority, a place organized for pleasure," and claiming that after Morgan and her sorors became engaged in curriculum planning they "dispensed with the usual pleasure program and set to work under the guidance of the Association for the Study of Negro Life and History and other agencies which could be induced to offer help."[22] The characterization of Phi Delta Kappa as unused to serious intellectual and social endeavors and in need of guidance was both flatly wrong and surprisingly misogynistic. Morgan and her sorors had conceived, planned, and executed the campaign that created the *Supplementary Units* themselves, and any suggestion that they had been spurred to action only "under the guidance" of the ASNLH was simply false. Such language also reflected an oft-expressed charge from some Black intellectuals that fraternity and sorority culture was insufficiently engaged in serious social and political work. Sociologist E. Franklin Frazier, for example, writing a decade later, would savage Black Greek letter organizations as the preserve of "social snobbishness" and "conspicuous consumption" as part of his larger critique of the vapidity and self-absorption he claimed characterized much of the Black middle class.[23] The fact that a similar critique of Black sororities found an audience in *NHB*, a publication deeply familiar with the educational work done by Black sororities, suggests that these types of generalizations were influential enough to penetrate even spaces where Black women held substantial amounts of power.

Certainly, Black sororities and fraternities at times displayed a sense of elitism, often centered on members' class background and color. However, such limited characterizations ignored the fact that social activism, particularly in the realm of education, had been a hallmark of Black Greek life for decades. For Black sorority members, many of whom pursued careers as teachers and school administrators, the connection was a natural one, and Black sororities supported various educational initiatives including the "funding of scholarships, schools, and colleges, as well as their support of specific causes related to education, such as desegregation and civil rights."[24] Zeta Phi Beta, for example, introduced scholarships and programs to combat juvenile delinquency; Alpha Kappa Alpha engaged in mentoring programs for youth; and the women of Delta Sigma Theta launched their May Week with its slogan of "Invest in Education" in order to "raise the consciousness of young people about the importance of higher education."[25] Morgan's own Phi Delta Kappa, specifically organized as a teaching sorority, funded a number of initiatives from scholarships for individual students to lectures for parents and community members. By setting Morgan and her sisters as a "noble example" that other "fraternal and quasi social organizations" would do well to emulate, the authors of the *NHB* piece assumed an apathy and inaction that did not actually characterize Black fraternities and sororities.[26]

The article continued its patronizing if positive tone in its assessment of Morgan's curriculum itself, noting that "some educators may not agree with the Chicago Bureau of Curriculum on all the methods suggested, and authorities in social science will question the omission of some data and the inclusion of facts which may be emphasized beyond their importance," before concluding that the work nevertheless amounted to an essential "broad foundation" that could be improved and added to over time. These comments, like those concerning Morgan's affiliation with Phi Delta Kappa, at least partially reflect the difficulty Black women found in receiving full endorsement for their work, even within their own race, an experience that both Morgan, her contemporaries, and many Black women scholars and educators in the present have widely shared.

Even within a publication largely produced by and dedicated to Black teachers and their work, Black schoolmen and especially schoolwomen working at the primary and secondary levels were often relegated to a somewhat ancillary position in the Black history movement. A 1945 article in the *NHB* written by none other than Carter G. Woodson makes this point more clearly. Woodson's piece, "Negro Historians of Our Time," surveys "a number of Negroes who may properly be designated as modern historians," lauding both the growth and the increasing professionalization of the field. Woodson concentrates on male academics, such as John Hope Franklin, Rayford Logan, and Luther P. Jackson, many of them financed by the association, along with a long list of other authors whose work delved into the Black past.[27]

Only toward the end of the piece does Woodson mention the work of Black teachers, noting that "this story would not be complete" without the inclusion of "at least certain men and women" who worked in "the adaptation of historical data to the capacity of school children." These figures included children's author Jane Dabney Shackelford, who received widespread praise for her historical work *The Child's Story of the Negro*, as well as her account of the day-to-day life of a contemporary Black family in *My Happy Days*; Helen A. Whiting, who authored the books *Negro Folk Tales* and *Negro Art, Music and Rhyme*; and Sadie Iola Daniel St. Clair, who wrote *Women Builders*.[28] While Woodson certainly supported Morgan and the efforts of schoolteachers more generally to popularize Black history, the distinction between mostly male academics and the female librarians, archivists, and teachers who supported, interpreted, contributed to, and expanded on their work kept Black women mostly relegated to the background as they were far less likely to gain entry into the formal scholarly community.[29]

Even though Morgan's work may not have received equal recognition from her male colleagues, the *NHB* was still an important outlet for her ideas. Although male authors wrote and contributed, the magazine was an especially vibrant forum for the voices of Black women teachers, who dominated its editorial staff and pages. Nowhere was this more evident than the Children's Page, begun in 1940, which included questions and facts about Black history and culture meant for use in primary and secondary classrooms. Proof that the Children's Page was written for teachers by teachers is that along with questions on Negro accomplishment and service throughout American history, the Children's Page also highlighted the efforts of important educators in the present, among them Madeline Morgan. Students in 1943 and 1944, for instance, were asked, "What can you say of the work of Madeline Morgan and Rachel C. McNeill? What are they trying to accomplish?" and "What do you know of such women as Volena G. Higginbotham, Constance Ridley Heslip, Jane Dabney Shackelford, and Madeline R. Morgan?"[30] The inclusion of Morgan in these questions reveals that for many of the female educators who staffed the *Bulletin* and created the Children's Page, Morgan was a figure with whom Black youth needed to be familiar.

At the same time, Morgan was also preparing to write another account of her work, this time appearing in a publication for a more scholarly audience, the *Journal of Negro Education (JNE)*. The *JNE* was launched a decade earlier in 1932 by the Howard University College of Education, the self-proclaimed "largest single group of professionally trained Negroes in the field of education in the United States."[31] The journal sought to create a nationally recognized space for the collection and dissemination of data on Black education, as well as analysis of programs and policies in the field. Morgan was approached by the publication in the summer of 1942 when the curriculum was first launched. Dr. Martin D. Jenkins, a Howard professor in educational psychology and a member of the journal's editorial staff, followed up with Morgan by letter that fall, reminding her of their earlier in-person conversation, and reiterating, "As I stated at that time, what we should like to have is an article concerning the Negro Achievement materials you assembled for use in the Chicago schools."[32] Jenkins detailed the proposed length of the article and some advice on what types of information might be most useful to the journal's readership.

Morgan's interactions with the *JNE* and her eventual publication in a winter 1944 piece titled "Chicago School Curriculum Includes Negro Achievements" put her on the radar of some of the nation's most prominent Black leaders.[33] The extent to which she was a subject of conversation can be seen in the letter of another prominent figure, labor leader Willard Townsend. Townsend was president of the United Transport Service Employees of America, a union that represented the interests of Black railway service workers, often better known as redcaps. By the mid-1940s he had transformed a single union in Chicago into a national brotherhood with representation in every major city in the country, an imprint that led to the growing union's affiliation with the larger Congress of Industrial Organizations, where Townsend became the first African American member of the CIO's general executive board. Townsend was energetic and passionate, his "itching foot" and "gregarious impulse" keeping him constantly on the move, negotiating, glad-handing, chiding, and exhorting, as the case and the audience demanded.[34] Yet, even amid this hectic existence, Townsend found his attention pulled to the schoolteacher from his adopted hometown whose work was quickly becoming a national sensation. Townsend wrote that as he crisscrossed the country he found himself "repeatedly asked" about Morgan and her work.[35] The final straw came as he visited Howard University, where historian Rayford Logan also asked Townsend to "tell him something about the program." Embarrassed, Townsend admitted to Morgan that his inability to speak to what was clearly a national topic of conversation made him feel "terribly guilty," and he admitted that "being so busily involved in ones [sic] own projects we are apt to become dismally ignorant of the things going on around us." Pledging to correct this mistake, the union head asked Morgan to forward him the curriculum, promising, like a student in one of her classes, to study it diligently in the weeks ahead.

One reason for Townsend's interest in Morgan and her work may have been his appointment to the newly formed Chicago Commission on Race Relations only months earlier. The commission, formed by Chicago's mayor, Robert Kelly, was a response to race riots that gripped the country throughout the summer of 1943, forcing cities across the nation to "look afresh at the acute problems in their midst."[36]

"*A Terrible Blow to the Morale of the American People*": Wartime Riots and White Educators' Responses to the Supplementary Units

The tensions that exploded into the streets between June and August 1943 had been building since the war began. The ongoing war effort led to massive internal migration within the US, as young men from various parts of the country relocated for basic training and military induction, and entire families moved to take advantage of work in the defense plants and shipyards of major cities. These relocations often dramatically reshaped the demographics of the urban environments where migrants arrived and exacerbated simmering racial tensions, with Black demands for access to fair employment, transportation, housing, public spaces, and education met with white resistance and violence. By the spring of 1943, several American cities were on the brink of implosion and needed only the slightest rumor or provocation to set off a serious clash. That summer, riots erupted in the production centers of Los Angeles; Detroit; Beaumont, Texas; and later Harlem. Smaller-scale clashes in Chester, Pennsylvania; Newark, New Jersey; Riverside, California; Augusta, Georgia; and elsewhere added to the hysteria. By the end of June, 23 Americans had lost their lives and 650 had been injured, with scores more left homeless or forced to flee.[37] In almost every case, these wartime riots were begun by white mobs intent on violently removing Black economic and social competition and stifling their opportunities in the defense industries.

The destruction unleashed in these attacks brought swift rebukes from a range of organizations, including the National Conference of Christians and Jews, the NAACP, the CIO, the United Automobile Workers, and the March on Washington Movement. The *Christian Science Monitor* echoed the sentiment of many of these groups when it declared that those responsible were un-American "seditionists," adding, "The riots in Los Angeles, Mobile, Beaumont, and Detroit killed scores, injured hundreds, and destroyed property worth millions of dollars. They caused serious losses to our production program [with 1,250,000 man hours lost in two days in Detroit alone], dealt a terrible blow to the morale of the American people, and provided the Axis with propaganda material which they have already put to deadly use."[38]

In response to the riots, both Black and white leadership called for calm, and local authorities rushed to enact measures to reduce racial animus. Along with calls for the prosecution of those responsible for provoking the unrest, interracial coalitions called for "the inauguration by the Government of an extensive, continuous campaign of public education in friendly relationships of mutual respect between members of majority and minority groups."[39] In this context, programs such as the one in Chicago were seen by many as a means of bettering race relations and preventing further damage to the war effort and American morale.

On June 21, 1943, only days after the riots in Beaumont killed two and injured sixty, and amid even more deadly unrest in Detroit, Morgan received her widest coverage to date, this time in the pages of *Time* magazine. The short feature, titled "Brown Studies," concentrated on how Morgan's materials were used to teach both "white and colored" students to respect one another and were "woven into the general class material." The article also described the woman behind the curriculum, emphasizing Morgan's youth and attractiveness, impeccable educational credentials, and above all her patriotism. A "handsome 36 year old Negro teacher" with a "master's degree in education from

Northwestern," Morgan fit easily into dominant notions of intellect and success.[40] By highlighting her focus on education, *Time* signaled to its largely white readership that despite the violence overwhelming the nation, a gradualist approach to race relations was still warranted.

In a similar vein, *PM*, a popular left-leaning newspaper based in New York City, put Morgan and her work directly into the context of the riots in September 1943.[41] The piece began, "After race riots in Detroit and elsewhere this Summer, the old ferment of discontent burbled ominously in Chicago's crowded Negro sections but there was no violence."[42] It is important to note that even in a liberal white publication that acknowledged the racial basis for the summer's riots, the concern quickly moved from white intransigence and violence to the "ominous" threat of Black retaliation. One explanation for the calm of Chicago's Black community, author Fletcher Wilson wrote, was the fact that leaders were relying on education "to remove the yokes of segregation and discrimination" and that "studies toward that end" had been "quietly introduced" into the public schools over the last year. The article went on to profile Morgan and her work, concentrating on the idea that the schools could "implant in minds young enough to be unconscious of color differences, an understanding that Negroes are no different than the red, brown, or white races" and that "such conditioning would be effective against development of prejudice in later years."[43] Education could be used to stem the tide of white racism and Black resentment, problems that Wilson and *PM* saw as equally vexing.

Like the *Time* article, *PM*'s story also presented Morgan as a model of Black restraint and respectability, a "cheerful, hopeful, handsome woman of 36" who lived in a "five room, tastefully furnished, ground floor apartment" in an "upper crust Negro neighborhood," and played tennis and piano in her time away from teaching duties. Although the article mentioned the discrimination she faced as a child, it assured readers she had conquered this animosity not through physical force or aggressive agitation but through her own "intellectual attainments and winsome personality." Similarly, as a teacher, Morgan was described as eschewing any connection to radicalism or violence. The article ended by stating that while "there are those in these uneasy times . . . who come to her and propose force to lift the Negro out of his status as a second-class citizen, [she] tells them uh-uh! Just give democratic educational tactics such as hers 20 years—one generation—on a national scale and antipathy to Negroes will disappear."

The presentation of Morgan in both *PM* and *Time* reveals much about the politics of representation faced by Black women in the 1940s. The riots of 1943 had overwhelmingly been initiated by white mobs angry over Black economic and social gains, and they threatened America's stability at home and victory abroad. Responses within the Black community ranged from demands for the prosecution of those responsible, to appeals to Americans of all stripes to uphold the nation's ideals and principles, to calls for violent retaliation. In the midst of these complex and complicated reactions, Morgan was presented in white publications as a voice for moderation. Her relative economic success and notoriety served as proof for white readers that progress was indeed possible, and that democratic and meritocratic traditions were more powerful than racism and prejudice. Her quiet manner, emphasis on education, and gradualist politics were put forward to soothe white anxieties.

It is difficult to assess Morgan's personal feelings about such presentation in white publications. In her interactions with the press she was unfailingly proper, demure, and personable. In many respects she embodied what scholar Evelyn Brooks Higginbotham described as the "politics of respectability," which served as both a shield against the charges of hypersexuality, ignorance, and uncleanliness regularly leveled against Black women of her time and a sword with which to assert their own equality, dignity, and worth.[44] However, as Higginbotham cautions, this conservative mode of self-presentation should not be mistaken for "an accommodationist stance towards racism, or a compensatory ideology in the face of powerlessness."[45] Morgan's propriety coexisted with a quiet but intense kind of radicalism, one that white journalists and observers were often incapable of seeing or unwilling to give credit. She was unwaveringly committed to full equality for Black people in every avenue of society, and the methods she employed to effect this change—organizing networks of activists and community institutions, producing and disseminating new knowledge, and taking powerful policy makers to task—spoke to her willingness to aggressively pursue these goals. White publications were not keen to depict Morgan in this more activist stance, and Morgan, for her part, seems not to have risked her larger work by challenging the conventional presentation of herself as a simple schoolmarm and her ideas as common sense and unthreatening. Yet her willingness to lean on the aspects of her personality that best fit societal expectations, and her choice to focus on "educational tactics," as opposed to "force," is not as straightforward as the *Time* and *PM* articles suggest. For Morgan, the classroom was not the opposite of street-level activism and protest; it was simply another front in the same struggle. Education was the theater of action she knew best, and the arena in which she could marshal her resources to greatest effect.

Although she consistently evinced a progressive's faith in the ability of pedagogy to change the underlying dynamics of social interactions, Morgan never assumed that this work would be easy or brief. As she warned, "erroneous concepts" about race were often "more steadfast than intellectual concepts" owing to the fact that they were deeply ingrained and constantly reinforced by the wider world.[46] Only a "difficult task of re-education," she surmised, could effectively chip away at this edifice of intolerance and bigotry. This constant work needed to be done "beginning in childhood" and continued diligently "through effective educational methods, year after year." Only then, Morgan insisted, would it lead to political and social change, as "the youth of today who will be in key positions fifteen or twenty years from now, will have a different attitude towards Negro Americans." Progress was not inevitable or assured, but Morgan chose to continue her work regardless.

However Morgan may have felt about the way in which she was covered by the press, there is no doubt that she put the added attention to immediate use. With the publication of the articles in *Time* and *PM*, she found herself inundated with requests as the 1943–44 school year began. Hundreds of letters to Morgan flooded in from across the country. By early 1944 she wrote in an article for the *Elementary English Review* that "forty states have been reached and almost a thousand sets of units have been mailed since September."[47] This increasing wave of requests included many white teachers, administrators, and policy makers seeking to employ Morgan's curriculum as part of their efforts to reduce racial tensions.

Laura J. Ladance, the principal of an integrated school in Dela-wanna, New Jersey, wrote to Morgan in the fall of 1943. Ladance had become familiar with Morgan from an article one of here teachers shared, and she was convinced by the Chicago educator's argument and methods. Landance began her letter by explaining that her town and school had a relatively small Black population, and that she be-lieved the twenty or so Black students under her charge were "very happy here because they are always treated the same as the other chil-dren, not only by the teachers but by the children themselves."[48] While she insisted that her school had what amounted to "a very happy sit-uation," however, Ladance revealed she and her staff had been put on edge by the disorders of the previous months "in other sections of the country," which left them "more anxious than ever to keep things on a harmonious basis." Here Ladance might have been referencing the events in Mobile, Los Angeles, New York, or Detroit. Yet a look closer to home reveals that just months prior to her letter, a series of clashes between white and Black youth in nearby Newark had led to several severe injuries and the killing of a fifteen-year-old Black student, Mil-ton Heiley, bringing the threat of disorder much closer.[49] Educators such as Ladance would have heard about this incident, which began at a citywide, multischool track meet before spilling out into the sur-rounding neighborhoods, where both sides armed themselves with "knives, clubs, and pistols" as the violence escalated.[50] Perhaps hoping to keep a similar situation from occurring in Delawanna, Ladance turned to Morgan and her work, hoping to incorporate the lessons into the larger curriculum of her building in a show of interracial unity. Speaking for herself and her staff, Ladance confided to Morgan that "very few of us know very much about 'Negro Culture,'" but she intimated that they were willing to try.[51] Apparently Morgan was also willing, as she jotted a note to herself at the top of Ladance's letter that read, "Units requested to be sent on Sept. 27–43."

If Ladance chose to tread lightly around the racial conflict and violence that underlay her request, others could not afford to be so delicate. School officials in the city of Los Angeles, for example, had seen some of the worst of that summer's disturbances. The West Coast of the United States was a critical location for military production, training, and defense of the home front against the possibility of Japanese aggression. These military prerogatives brought thousands of servicemen, most of them white, to the cities of Los Angeles, San Diego, and other communities in Southern California. In Los Angeles, these personnel met and often clashed with Black and Mexican American youth, who had long-established claims to the city's street corners, movie houses, bars, and other gathering spots. Throughout the early war years, tensions escalated. Then, in the summer of 1943, violence exploded into the streets.

From June 3 to 8, the city of Los Angeles was the site of massive rioting as white servicemen from the surrounding bases repeatedly descended onto Mexican American and African American neighborhoods intent on destruction and violence. The conflagration became known as the Zoot Suit Riots, a reference to the bold fashion sported by Mexican American and African American youth and supposedly connected to criminal activity, but that name inaccurately shifts the blame to minority youth instead of the white military personnel who initiated and continued the violence. Far from protecting themselves from delinquents as they would later claim, white rioters were the aggressors in most cases, indiscriminately attacking Black and Brown youth. The failure of the military to control the rioting and the "apparent approval of law enforcement and the press" meant that the violence stretched over a full week before the navy issued orders to restrict enlisted men from the Los Angeles area and control was restored. As the racially fueled riots spread and gained intensity, African Americans were often targeted alongside Mexican Americans by the ire of white sailors and marines.[52]

As the smoke cleared from the riots, many asked what might be done to prevent the city from again falling victim to mob violence. School officials, among others, were tasked with combating the racial prejudice that helped create the conditions for the riots. In this atmosphere, Morgan and her work were sought out as an example of what was possible. On November 29, 1943, Robert Hill Lane, the assistant superintendent of the Los Angeles Public Schools, wrote simply:

> Here in Los Angeles, with its tremendous Negro problem, we have heard of your success in developing work units for children which reflect the achievement of the Negroes during the past two decades.
>
> We are very anxious to see and use your materials. May we have copies?[53]

For Lane and the Los Angeles Board of Education, the *Supplementary Units* were part of the effort to restore calm and show that the schools had taken some measure of action in the aftermath of the riots, which involved and impacted many of the city's youth. Yet Lane's reference to the "Negro problem" betrayed his and the school board's unwillingness to assign blame to the white officers and enlisted men who had initiated the violence, and his desperation to make the riots somehow the fault of their Black and Brown victims.

As unsettling as the violence in Los Angeles and elsewhere in the early summer of 1943 proved, the riots that gripped Detroit from June 20 to 22 brought an unprecedented level of destruction and loss of life. While racial tensions had been present in Detroit for decades, it was the city's prominent role in war production as the "leading symbol of the Arsenal of Democracy" that exposed already-festering indignities and created new conflicts.[54] From 1940 to 1943, fifty thousand

Black migrants and half a million whites migrated to Detroit for employment. As Black people attempted to gain equal opportunities for employment, adequate housing, decent schools, and access to parks and playgrounds, they often met with white resistance. This resistance came in the form of strikes at defense plants and white improvement associations focused on the obstruction of their efforts. Prime examples of this resistance were the violence that surrounded the construction of the Sojourner Truth public housing project in 1942, which resulted in massive protests by white communities in which several were injured, and the state was forced to deploy the National Guard to ensure that Black residents were able to occupy their homes. This incident was followed in 1943 by a twenty-five-thousand-man strike by white workers in retaliation for the promotion of Black employees at a Packard plant. These outbursts were not relegated to adults. White youth gangs policed racial borders within and between neighborhoods, and clashes between groups of white and Black youth appeared in newspaper headlines on an almost weekly basis.[55]

By the summer of 1943 tensions had reached a tipping point. On Sunday, June 20, a fight at Belle Isle, a local amusement park, spiraled into all-out rioting as competing rumors spread through both Black and white communities throughout the night. By that Monday morning the chaos had reached its full intensity as mobs of rioters fought with knives, bricks, and guns. Stores were looted, public transportation lines were attacked and finally shut down, and schools closed as students were "kept home by frightened parents . . . or taken home as word of the rioting spread."[56] Although city and state officials had been repeatedly warned of the possibility of such violence for months, the response was both wholly inadequate and ineptly administered, contributing to further bloodshed. In addition, the city's police force, almost all white, tacitly and sometimes openly encouraged the violence of white mobs while responding to Black looters with deadly force. By the time federal troops were finally called into the city to restore order, 34 people had been killed (25 of them Black and 17 of those shot by the Detroit police), an additional 500 injured, and 1,800 arrested.[57]

Both civic and civil rights groups grappled with what might be done to limit the threat of another explosion. Part of the response centered on the schools, with intercultural education seen as a key component in building understanding between the races. On November 2, 1943, this conviction led to the creation of the Administrative Committee on Intercultural and Interracial Education, chaired by the superintendent of Detroit's public schools, Paul Rankin. The committee, along with some two hundred smaller committees at individual school sites, acted to facilitate the "special responsibility" of the schools in "developing in children and adults the knowledge, understanding, and attitudes that make for good race relations."[58] This responsibility was carried out through four main channels, including "curriculum, continued education of teachers, organization and administration, and school community relations." Working with organizations such as the Detroit Interracial Committee, the Committee on Interracial Understanding in the Schools, the Intercultural Council of Southeast Michigan, the Board of Education Speakers' Bureau, and the Program for Vocational Training for War Production Workers, along with various parent-teacher associations, the committee developed workshops and training sessions, brought in speakers, and held town halls and community conferences, eventually developing an intercultural education plan that merited national recognition. Among the initiatives Detroit educators touted were the preparation of Negro History Week bulletins to be used in all schools, the adoption of pamphlets like *Becoming One Nation Indivisible*, and the creation of lists of best practices and examples of intercultural education strategies including "units of study" along with "extra curricular activities, school newspapers, visual materials, radio programs, and the like," which provided exemplary materials from which Detroit teachers could draw inspiration.

As leaders in Detroit searched for the means to initiate a program in intercultural education, they also sought out the advice of recognized experts in the field on a national level. As historians Anne-Lise Halvorsen and Jeffrey Mirel have written, much of this effort revolved around Rachel Davis DuBois and her Bureau for Intercultural

Education in New York, which sent representatives such as Margaret Mead, Charles S. Johnson, and Hilda Taba to Detroit as consultants.[59] Yet the Administrative Committee on Intercultural and Interracial Education also looked to other groups and individuals, studying their "plans and procedures," and was particularly drawn to the work done in two regions of the country: Springfield, Massachusetts, and Chicago.[60] As a result, a letter from Marion Edwan, an associate professor at Wayne State University and a member of the administrative Committee, found its way to Madeline Morgan on February 8, 1944. In the letter, Edwan expressed a desire to take advantage of an upcoming trip to Chicago for a meeting of the American Association of School Administrators in order to "visit some of the work being done along inter-cultural lines in Chicago."[61] Edwan asked Morgan for her help in identifying "the types of activities" that would be "most worthwhile" for him and other members of the committee to see in action, and he suggested a meeting between the committee members, Morgan, and Charlemae Rollins of the Chicago Public Libraries, Morgan's long-time ally. Edwan assured Morgan that he would be "deeply indebted to you for any help or suggestions which you can give us." Morgan's imprint made it to the final versions of the Detroit committee's plan, where she is listed among the panel of thirteen experts consulted for the project, an indication of the extent to which her expertise and advice were sought in this and similar projects.

"For the Better World in the Making": The Reach of the Supplementary Units

In the period between 1942 and 1945, Madeline Morgan and the curriculum she authored were part of national conversations about race, history, democracy, and education. They were recognized by the Black community as a powerful example of the possibility of extending Black history into the mainstream of American life. In addition, especially in the wake of the 1943 riots, her work was considered by a growing number of liberal white educators and policy makers a vital part of the effort to hold together a nation tearing at the political and ideological seams. Beyond schools and school district leadership, Morgan also received requests from a mix of religious and civil rights organizations including the National Conference of Christians and Jews in New York, the Maine Unitarian Association in Kennebunk, the Sheil School of Social Studies in Chicago, and the Phyllis Wheatley Settlement House in Minneapolis. As Morgan wrote in a piece for the *Elementary English Review,* "Among some of those receiving units are people as far south as South America; as far north as Maine; as far West as California; as distant as Italy and Africa; and the United States Office of Education in Washington D.C., boards of education, social agencies, ministers, principals, teachers, soldiers, colleges, city interracial commissions, and interested citizens."[62]

One such request came from Morton Brooks, a white serviceman, who wrote to Morgan on December 16, 1943, from a military base in Italy. The September 6 issue of *PM,* which contained the profile of Morgan, had finally reached the front, some three months after its initial publication. As Brooks read through the "usual complement of interesting and informative features," he was struck by the article devoted to the teacher from Chicago and "the inspiring work you have been doing in the field of race relations."[63] As he explained to Morgan, he had given the article a good deal of thought and was compelled to write because he was caretaker for two nieces, Barbara, age nine, and Ann, age twelve, back home in New York. The girls were growing up without his influence as he served abroad, and as events both at home and overseas intensified, he worried that they might be influenced by the racial bigotry and hatred they saw around them: "Right now they are forming impressions of their world which will color their outlook throughout adult life. It is at this age that principles are inculcated— principles or prejudices. I am, naturally, very anxious that my nieces grow up to be persons of principle, not of prejudice." If he were with them, Brooks explained, he would be more confident in their becoming young women of character, but the war left him "too far in space and time to explain what must seem to them strange and disturbing in their expanding universe." Letters alone, he worried, were no use, as

he sounded "preachy and dull even to my own ears." Instead, he hoped
Morgan might help. He begged her to send,

> either directly to them or to me, copies of your pamphlets on
> Negro history—the same pamphlets that have had such wonder-
> ful results in the Chicago schools. For the younger girl I think
> the fourth to sixth grade of books is appropriate, for the older, I
> suggest the more advanced one, used in grades seven and eight. If
> you think the pamphlets would not make suitable reading for the
> children themselves, send them to me and I shall incorporate the
> information they contain into my letters home.

Brooks ended his letter by hoping confidently for a response. After
all, both of them, he believed, were "workers, each in his own way, for
the better world in the making."[64]

Brooks's letter brings our attention out of the realm of policy prescriptions and national movements, squarely back to the effects of
Morgan's work on the students who read and engaged with it in the
mid-1940s. While Brooks wrote to Morgan out of concern for only
the two young persons in his charge, he turned to Morgan because
she was "helping to educate the many children of a great city." It is to
these children we turn next, to ask how Morgan's work was taught and
understood by white and Black teachers and students in the classroom.

Madeline Morgan (speaking), with Bessie Smith, Elinor McCollom, and Supt. William H. Johnson (seated at left), at a dinner celebrating the Supplementary Units, 1942.

CHAPTER 5

"ERASE THE COLOR LINE FROM THE BLACKBOARDS OF AMERICA"

The *Supplementary Units* in the Classroom

$\mathcal{D}$ECEMBER 16, 1943—"Read it again, please."[1]

The students of Grace Markwell's social studies class were held in "rapt attention."[2] Ms. Markwell, who taught fifth, sixth, and seventh grades at S. E. Gross Elementary in the lily-white suburb of Brookfield, Illinois, had chosen this day to introduce new material to her course. When her fifth-grade class covered the industrial revolution of the nineteenth century, Markwell included a short passage on Jan Matzeliger, the inventor of Dutch and African descent who had pioneered the shoe lasting machine. The story of a "Negro inventor," something that her students had never imagined existed, left at least one class quite literally speechless. The children sat groping for words, until a single student recovered enough composure to make a request to hear the entire story over again, which the teacher readily obliged. However, Markwell was not quite finished pushing her students' boundaries. She compounded their surprise with even more substantial revelations: the author of the passage was also Black, a woman named Madeline Morgan, and she hailed from just a few miles to the east in the city of Chicago. Perhaps most shocking to the children was that Markwell, a personal friend of Morgan's who had even dined at her home, could attest that beyond being an accomplished writer and teacher, Morgan was incidentally a "very good cook when it came to bacon and eggs." At this her students launched into a flurry of questions: "Are there really Negro teachers?" "What are they like?" "Does she talk over the radio?" "Does she talk to schools?" "Could she talk to us?" Markwell eventually conceded that a class letter was necessary. Her fifth-grade students penned the following:

Dear Miss Morgan,

Miss Markwell read us the story you wrote about Jan Matzeliger. We enjoyed it very much. Then she read us a story about you and we think your contribution is as important as those about which you have written, because you are helping children of your race be proud of their color and helping us to want to help give them a chance to learn, to work and to show what they can do.

When Miss Markwell told us that she knew you we were surprised and delighted [to] think that she knew someone so famous. We know that you are very busy, but we wish you to know that our class would like to know you and to thank you personally for writing the stories.

We have school [all] next week except Friday. If you have vacation then, and can spare a little time, you will find a warm welcome in Gross School. If you can come, let us know when you will arrive and we will meet you at the station.

Sincerely yours,

Fifth Grade—Room 214

By late 1943, fewer than two years after it was published, Morgan's work had already been highly successful in terms of its recognition and endorsement, both by the general public and by other educators. Its adoption as part of the curriculum of Chicago's public schools, and its use as a template and inspiration for efforts in districts throughout the country, was a testament to the combination of her own singular determination and the shifting politics of race and representation during the war years. However, as Markwell's class reminds us, the success of Morgan's mission ultimately depended on its reception at the classroom level by individual teachers and students. Morgan's desire to "extend information about Negro Americans" to as wide an audience as possible flowed from three interrelated goals. First, Morgan aimed to make Black audiences in particular "proud of their cultural heritage."[3] Black children lived under a constant and pervasive barrage of racist imagery from children's literature, songs, films, newspapers, and other popular media. School texts reinforced these messages through the "blatant dismissal of African Americans' historical experiences" and "outwardly racist depictions" of Black people from slavery up to the present day.[4] Through the *Supplementary Units* Morgan countered these prevalent negative stereotypes.

Second, Black history would not only serve as a vindication of the past but also constitute a necessary prelude to social, economic, and political recognition in the present. As she put it in a speech in 1943, "What does the Negro want? It is this. Negro Americans want justice. He wants the right to work and raise himself to a higher economic standard. He wants to enjoy the dignity of being a man among men . . . an equal chance as an American citizen to pursue his chosen fields."[5] A knowledge of Black history, in Morgan's view, could make Black youth better equipped to claim this "equal chance," to work toward the full inclusion they were entitled to as American citizens. As she would put it decades later, she strove to show that Black people did not need to "earn the right to citizenship in this land that we have already helped to develop."[6]

Lastly, looking beyond the Black community, Morgan also argued that Black history could act to reduce the racial antipathy of white students, offering an early inoculation against the prejudice that surrounded them. Just as an appreciation of Black history would bolster Black students' confidence in their own calls for equality, Morgan believed that white audiences would come to recognize the legitimacy of Black claims to full citizenship when confronted with evidence of

Black achievement and advancement. For Morgan, as for many of the liberal educators of her day—both Black and white—anti-Black prejudice and racism were deeply rooted in ignorance and miseducation. Her mentor Carter G. Woodson, for example, believed fervently that racism was "not something inherent in human nature" but instead "the logical result of tradition, the inevitable outcome of thorough instruction that the Negro has never contributed anything to the progress of mankind."[7] Yet this process could also be reversed, since "just as a thorough education in the inequality of the races has brought the world to the cat and dog stage of religious and racial strife, so may a thorough education in the equality of races bring about a reign of brotherhood." Because the absence of accurate information allowed bigotry to spread unchecked, educators had a responsibility to their knowledge of history record to stop the spread of racial hatred. Echoing this sentiment, Morgan wrote:

> Intolerance toward Negroes is caused by incomplete views. The underlying facts involved are seldom presented, and students are not aroused to a real point of interest. Student opinions and attitudes are fundamentally determined by their parents or the social group in which they live and the truth about the path over which they have traveled is unknown to them.[8]

Morgan's answer, like Woodson's, was to replace ignorance and misinformation with fact. By reaching white youth before prejudice became cemented as part of their worldview, Morgan believed educators could mold a new generation with "a different attitude towards Negro Americans." Following progressive ideals, Morgan deemed the schoolroom the natural place to take up such a project of societal transformation and make real the promise of American democracy.

Measuring the extent to which these ideas made it to the classroom, and how they were received there, is a challenging task. The day-to-day thoughts of teachers and students are not often preserved and archived as the stuff of history. In the case of Morgan's *Supplementary*

Units, however, there are a few surviving materials, including, most importantly, student reactions from both Black and white classrooms, that point to the ways in which teachers and students engaged with Morgan's work. These pieces of evidence show us something of the strengths and limitations of Morgan's model, and of tolerance education more broadly.

"But We Still Haven't Got All Our Rights and That's That": *Black Students and the* Supplementary Units

For African American youth, the *Supplementary Units* were intended first and foremost as a means of making visible the Black presence in American history, something almost entirely absent from the curricular discourses of the period. As Morgan and King tested their materials with Black audiences, they noted that for many students, seeing the names and exploits of African Americans was something completely novel in their schooling and acted to strengthen their self-image. Morgan and King reported that common reactions of Black students included statements such as "I am proud to know that I am Negro," "We feel uplifted when we learn our race is doing something," and "We don't need to feel ashamed of the Negro race."[9] Seventh-grade student James Williams remarked that "when I read in books about Negros and what they has done I feel that the Negro has did a great deal in the making of our country."[10]

Students not only expressed pride in gaining knowledge about the contributions of Black Americans to national life and history, they also identified these accomplishments as part of their own stories and identities, the units allowed them to see themselves in the curriculum for the first time, as would later ethnic studies, Afrocentric, and multicultural education movements in the decades to come.[11] Morgan and King actively drew this connection between history and the present day, stating, "There are many European groups who came to America to live. All of them know something about their ancestors and the countries from which they came. They are justly proud of their heritage. However, for so long Africa was the dark continent, little was known about the lives of the ancestors of the American Negro. Now that more is known we can learn more about them."[12] Student Robert Miller encapsulated this feeling when he wrote, "I feel proud of the negro people and what all they have done. I feel that I was some part of them."[13] Similarly, eighth-grade student Mary Thomas wrote, "When I hear or read about good things about the Negro it make me feel proud to hear the name that I too, Mary Thomas, am a Negro too."[14] For students like Robert and Mary, the *Supplementary Units* represented not only a chance to learn about new figures and ideas but also an invitation to claim themselves as important actors in the drama of the American story for the first time. As another student, Sandra Clark, explained:

> Since I have studied Negro history every good word about Negroes and also good thing they do make me feel swell. Just to think at one time we were only allowed to do nothing but work night and day and did not know where we would be the next night because the master might sell you to someone else. and now today we are doing things as import[ant] as anybody else it would make anybody feel swell if it were people who were of the same race or creed that you are.[15]

Clark's contrast between the past, in which slavery deprived Black Americans of control over their bodies, labor, and lives, and the present, in which she could envision not only surviving but thriving, provides a deeply moving testament to how some students interacted with the *Supplementary Units*.

This bridging of past and present was also shown in the ways students grappled with the war and its implications for racial equality. Black youth in Chicago found every facet of their lives deeply impacted by the war effort. They donated canned goods and scrap metal, bought war bonds and stamps, and practiced civilian defense drills in their Boy Scout and Girl Scout troops. They listened to radio broadcasts that dramatized the role of Black people in the military. They whistled and waved as the annual Bud Billiken parade, the largest celebration of Black community and culture in the city if not the country, was transformed into a "March for Victory."[16] Through these and other means, Black youth imagined themselves as equal citizens and dreamed of a postwar world in which democracy triumphed both at home and abroad. In this context the *Supplementary Units* were a means of articulating a Black American vision of equal citizenship. Through its coverage of past military heroes like Austin Dabney and Crispus Attucks, and more contemporary ones like the veterans of the Illinois Eighth Infantry, Morgan's curriculum refuted the logic of Black inferiority and challenged the discrimination and second-class citizenship endured by Black Americans.

Responses written by Morgan's students attest to the fact that they saw Black soldiers enlisting and fighting in the current war as taking up this heroic mantle. Several of the surviving pieces of student writing mesh pride in Black historical and contemporary accomplishments with an equal amount of enthusiasm about the African American contribution to the war. For instance, student William Roy Young's response referred proudly to Benjamin O. Davis; the Ninety-Ninth Pursuit Squadron, the pioneering unit of Black airmen trained at Tuskegee Institute whose recruitment, training, and exploits were covered extensively in the Black press; and boxing champion Joe Louis, whose enlistment in the US Army and subsequent appearances in film, radio, and poster campaigns helped popularize the war effort to Black audiences and especially young people.[17] Another student, Jim Mitchell, explicitly connected Black history to the war effort:

> I feel great when I hear how our Negro men and women help put us out of slave's and build this great nation. I feel good about the 99 sq. The way they are help fighting this war. And it is very good to know that it was a Negro doctor who first operated on a person. And its [*sic*] good to know that Joe Louis is [the] greatest fighter in the world. And our great singe[r] Mary [*sic*] Anderson who have the best voice know in world. And General Davis first Negro General in the Army.[18]

The *Supplementary Units* gave some Black students a context in which to place their personal experience of the war as well. Millie Rogers wrote: "It makes me feel proud to know that our boys are in the fight. And not just the white people. I have people in the war. I know that they are fighting somewhere. And when the war is over everyone will come home."[19] The mix of anxiety and pride that accompanied having "people in the war" would have been a shared experience for many of Morgan's students, whose brothers, uncles, and fathers had either volunteered or were drafted.

Throughout the war, Morgan also received correspondence from several former pupils, a testament to just how recent their school days were for many GIs. In these letters, past students often connected their current military service to the larger effort to defeat racial prejudice at home and praised Morgan's work on this second front. Writing from France, a soldier named J. Burns observed that based on what he had read and heard, his old teacher "must be doing a good piece of work in spreading the gospel of tolerance," adding, "more power to you."[20] Another former student wrote from England that he hoped Morgan was "still engaged in spreading goodwill among the races" and proclaimed that both his efforts and hers would help the country "march to final victory!"[21] A third, George M. Cooper, observing the mayor's official pronouncement observing Negro History Week in 1945, remarked, "I picture you as one of the people who have shown the world that the Negro has a history and has shown them that it should be known to everyone including the Negro."[22]

Perhaps the clearest example of the ways in which ideas about education, citizenship, history, and the war effort intersected, however, came from a soldier whom Morgan did not know, a Pvt. Edward Butler, who wrote from North Africa to request copies of the *Supplementary Units*. His letter read:

> Dear Mrs. Morgan,
> I just read an article about you and your work I writting [sic] to you to find out if I can get a copy of the Negroes History which

was mention in Newsreel Magazine it is something I didn't learn
in school. But would like to learn it now I'll be glad when we are
called Brown Soldier instead of Negrosoldier We are fighting and
working for the same cause as every one [else] from the States
    Your[s] Until,
    Edward[23]

Like Morgan's students at Emerson, Butler connected the desire
to learn about his past to his role as a "Brown Soldier." While it was
true that he was fighting for the "same cause as everyone else from
the States," soldiers like Butler were also struggling for a particular
freedom of their own.

The *Supplementary Units* bolstered the pride of many Black students
in their contributions to the war effort and to American history writ
large. Yet for others, like Carroll Campbell, the *Supplementary Units*
brought to mind not only the role Black Americans played in the
defense of the country but also the unequal treatment they received
despite their sacrifices. In a response that paralleled sentiments expressed in the Black press and elsewhere, she wrote: "I feel proud to
know what [our] boys are doing, but when I think about what hap-
pen[ed] in the last war Its of fact they promise our race jobs and a lot
of other things which they did not [give] they would not even let the
Color[ed] race stay in the navy."[24]

Throughout US history, Black soldiers had faced the paradox of
defending the freedoms of others while simultaneously being denied
rights themselves. As scholars Anthony Brown, Ryan Crowley, and
LaGarrett King state, "A key component of the notion of the citizen-
soldier is that the service and sacrifice he provides earns him something in return. . . . In death, his name is memorialized. In life, he often
gains access to parts of society that were previously closed to him."[25]
Yet as Campbell pointed out in her response, Black soldiers had been,
time after time, denied the legal protection, economic access, civic
acknowledgment, and social equality warranted by their service. Thus,
her enthusiasm and pride in knowing "what our boys are doing" was

tempered by the realization that these efforts had not yet brought about a change in conditions for Black America.

Another student, Louis Brown, mirrored Campbell's assertion that the country still owed much to its Black citizens and soldiers alike. He wrote, "The way I feel about this thing is I feel that Negroes are just as hep as any other race and can do if they will. And I think we should get just as good a brake as anybody else. . . . But we still haven't got all our rights and that's that."[26] In truly sophisticated ways, students like these were using history as a starting point to think about their position as citizens. By insisting on the value and significance of the Black contributions to the nation in both the past and the present, Morgan had created an intellectual space where students could set the record of Black achievement against the current treatment they received in American life. For students like Louis and Carroll, America's promise of equality and democracy was tried and found wanting.

Overall, Black students recognized the *Supplementary Units* as something new and welcome in their experience of history and of education more broadly. Reading about Black historical contributions and current sacrifices offered a clear rebuttal to narratives of Black incapacity or inferiority and allowed Black students to assert their own worth and dignity along with that of their race. As student Mary Ann Jones put it, the stories she read about Black history proved, "We [Black Americans] have as much brain or maybe more than a White man" and left her determined to "show the White man what a Negro can do."[27] Another student wrote that each time he heard something positive about his people it made him feel "that negro people are doing something also to make American one of the greatest country" before adding, "I feel that when I am a man negro people will have the right[s] and freedom and I hope I am able to help in anyway them along somehow."[28] Barbara Hariston summed up her feelings in this way:

> I feel when I hear good things about my race that we too can hold our head up and say we [are] proud. Because we Can think and say that one of Our own schoolteachers help bring Negro History in

America. And there not another person on earth whether he Black, white, or any other color can be any better than the Negro race. America history has now begun and we'll [be] proud because we have kinfolks also fighting [for] Democracy and dying for each and every one of us.[29]

Measured by these responses, Morgan accomplished her goal of instilling pride in Black youth by helping them become more knowledgeable concerning their past. Additionally, she sparked their thinking about the challenges and potential of the present moment.

"Maybe White Children Will Become More Tolerant When They Study the Achievements of the Negro": The Supplementary Units *in the White Classroom*

The reactions of Black students to the *Supplementary Units* varied from pride in Black accomplishment to anger over the barriers still faced by African Americans. White students and teachers engaged with Morgan's curriculum in equally interesting and complicated ways. While the units had been adopted as part of Chicago's curriculum, they remained an addendum to the regular course of instruction, and there is no evidence that teachers, white or Black, received much official incentives or support or incentive to incorporate the materials into their lessons. Those white teachers who did adopt and use the *Supplementary Units* were those who decided for themselves, whether through personal conviction or professional interest, that Black history should be woven into their existing studies. The reactions of these educators, although a minority, allow us to see how the units were implemented by white teachers dedicated to developing intercultural understanding.

One commonality between both Black and white classrooms was the intense interest students displayed toward the content. In their initial tests of the materials with students, Morgan and King recorded that "both white and colored children were eager to hear the stories and were surprised to learn that Negroes had made so many contributions to the development of American life." As one teacher remarked,

"When I read the stories about Negroes my room is as quiet as death. The children simply love the units."[30] This interest often extended beyond the bounds of the classroom and the capacities of white teachers, necessitating the creation of new spaces and continued conversations. As another reported, "The students knew so little about Negroes they were inspired to do research on their own. They wanted to talk about Negroes all day every day. I couldn't do that so I had to organize a Negro History Club. I asked the students to save their findings and questions either for the regular daily history period or the weekly Negro history club."

In addition, like Black students who saw in the accomplishments of earlier generations an argument against their own disenfranchisement, white students connected the Black history they learned to the need for racial tolerance in the present. The same teacher remarked that while studying the theme of tolerance in a separate lesson, one of her students stated, "Maybe white children will become more tolerant when they study the achievements of the Negro." The comment embodied Morgan's hope that an increased knowledge of Black history could legitimate calls for racial equality claims in the eyes of young white audiences.

"I Have Never Been Able to Achieve the Success in Changing Attitudes That Resulted from the Use of the Supplementary Units*": Grace Markwell and Madeline Morgan*

The most detailed account of the use of the *Supplementary Units* in a white classroom comes from Grace Markwell, an elementary school teacher in Brookfield, Illinois. Markwell, like Morgan, was a veteran social studies teacher with a marked interest in the topic of race relations.

The path leading Markwell to the teaching of Black history and eventually to Madeline Morgan began with her involvement with the Illinois Council for the Social Studies (ICSS). The ICSS was a state-level affiliate of the National Education Association's National Council for the Social Studies (NCSS). Composed of public school teachers, principals, and district administrators, along with college professors from schools of education across the country, the NCSS was an influential and important organization that impacted classroom practice through its meetings as well as publications, resource lists for teachers and administrators, special bulletins, curricula, and yearbooks.

Since the beginning of the war, the NCSS had committed itself to adapting the teaching of social studies to meet the challenges of the ongoing conflict. Convinced that "the stamina of a fighting democracy depends on the widespread understanding of the issues at stake, of the stark necessities of total war on a global scale, and the complex task of achieving a peace," the NCSS established a Committee on Wartime Policy that worked to engage social studies educators toward the goal of total victory.[31] The organization instructed teachers to think of themselves as responsible for the "mobilization of minds" both in the classroom and in the larger community, and argued that "teachers of social studies have an urgent duty in helping to form today's opinion as well as instructing tomorrow's citizen." This duty was reflected throughout the council's wartime policy, including its stance on race relations.

The mobilization plan of the NCSS included several priorities: increasing civics education in order to stress the "contrasts between dictatorship and democracy"; strengthening the teaching of geography in order to give students an understanding of the "far flung action of American troops"; expanding work in economics to explain topics like rationing and price controls; and encouraging students in the "careful use of personal possessions, school supplies, and public property."[32] In addition, the organization promoted the teaching of racial and religious unity as a means of decreasing conflict during war and winning the peace that would follow. In its statement of wartime policy, the NCSS included a section with the heading "Racial and National Hatreds Must Be Attacked" and offered strategies for its members that reflected the growing emphasis on tolerance education. They encouraged the "systematic study of the achievements and contributions to our national life and to world civilization of representative races and nationalities" and the recruitment of minority "resource persons" who would acquaint teachers and students with "the points of view, cultural contributions, and problems of their groups."[33] As with the larger tolerance movement, the NCSS program was primarily concerned with altering the feelings of white students and meant primarily to build their "friendliness towards other people" and their appreciation of "the rich heritage of music, arts, crafts, traditions, literature, and other aspects of culture which each immigrant group has brought with it to American shores."[34] The push for "harmonious race relations" was reflected in the classroom projects and priorities taken up at the local level eventually leading Grace Markwell to Morgan and the *Supplementary Units.*

Markwell believed that preparing her white students to respect difference was part of both her civic and moral duty. She became part of the ICSS elementary committee in 1943 and suggested a project on "the promotion of better racial understanding through interracial cooperation."[35] As the previous chapter makes clear, civil disturbances and full-scale riots during the summer of 1943 had focused the attention of the tolerance education movement squarely on the relationship between Black and white Americans.[36] Markwell, like many liberal whites, was convinced that "the Negro, through no fault of his own," constituted "one of the major challenges on the home front."[37] Frustrated that the work of race relations was being conducted in an echo chamber of white teachers, Markwell complained, "I have listened to panels, roundtables, seminars, lectures, and just plain discussions on the subject and, in most cases, it has been a group of our own race, trying in our isolation, to solve the problem." She suggested instead that the ICSS make an attempt to find Black teachers who could partner in this work. Her request brought her more than she bargained for, as ICSS president Robert S. Ellwood accepted her suggestion but put Markwell in charge of both the committee itself and finding Black educators who might be amenable. Overwhelmed and possessed of far more enthusiasm than expertise, Markwell admitted that when it came to intercultural relations, she "knew absolutely nothing of the subject." She nevertheless proceeded, intent on finding "some sympathetic Negro teacher who would work with us." Fortunately for Markwell, the search did not last long. Her inquiries were met time and again with references to Morgan, who by then had received extensive attention in both academic and popular circles. Intent on securing her help, Markwell added herself to the long list of educators seeking Morgan's expertise.

Morgan and Markwell first met in the fall of 1943 at Morgan's home in Chicago. The fact that it was Morgan and not Markwell who dictated the location made clear that Markwell would need to put herself in unfamiliar territory both intellectually and geographically. As Morgan remembered: "It was during the course of one of our chats that Miss Markwell invited me to her home. But when she confessed that her knowledge of the South Side was limited to reaching the University of Chicago, I replied, 'Your education has been sorely neglected, therefore I am inviting you to have coffee with me at my home Saturday morning.'"[38]

Markwell knew virtually nothing about Bronzeville, what she called the "Negro district," and had admittedly "never been in a colored home." However uncomfortable she may have been at first, she quickly found a rapport with her host as Morgan cooked breakfast and the pair discussed her plans for the committee and their teaching more broadly. Taken aback by the depth of Morgan's expertise, Markwell admitted, "I never felt quite so incompetent before." The two found much to bond over, most significantly that both evinced a shared faith in the power of pedagogy to bring about social change. As Markwell wrote, "Both of us, quite naturally for teachers, feel that the school is our greatest hope."[39]

Beyond their shared calling, the two women enjoyed somewhat similar backgrounds and worldviews. As Markwell stated about Morgan and two other Black teachers who joined the NCSS committee at Morgan's behest, "Color . . . was about the only real difference between us. Professionally, culturally, and in religious training we had much in common."[40] Although these shared professional and personal values did not, and indeed could not, make race "immaterial," as Markwell hoped, they undoubtedly gave the two teachers shared points of reference. For Markwell, Morgan's middle-class values and propriety made their camaraderie all the easier. Reflecting the mixture of racial openness and social elitism that characterized much of the interracial organizing among women of the period, Markwell wrote, "If we make opportunities to associate with colored people of similar interests and cultural background, we are surprised at the ease with which our interest turns to friendship."[41] While the "distancing impact" of segregation meant Black and white women, even those with similar class and social backgrounds, lived in largely separate worlds, middle-class women of both races occasionally crossed the color line, forming coalitions aimed at education, uplift, and interracialism.[42] While by no means free of their own level of prejudice and racial bias, spaces like the Young Women's Christian Association, Girl Scouts, and Committee for Interracial Cooperation offered opportunities for Black and white women to develop professional and personal relationships while fighting for shared causes. The ICSS Intercultural Relations committee became such a venue for Markwell and Morgan, who recognized their common interests and decided to combine their separate efforts to achieve similar ends.

By the end of breakfast that first morning, Morgan had been convinced to join Markwell on the ICSS committee, and as the two continued their friendship and collaboration, Markwell began to incorporate the material from the *Supplementary Units* into her courses, leaving a detailed account of how intercultural education sounded and looked in an all-white environment. Markwell found that the stories and excerpts from the *Supplementary Units* elicited a strong response from her classes. As she put it, "I have always hoped that I was creating an appreciation for peoples of cultures differing from our own, but I have never been able to achieve the success in changing attitudes that resulted from the use of the 'Supplementary Units.'"[43]

In keeping with the practices suggested by organizations like the NCSS and Bureau for Intercultural Education, Markwell surveyed her students' opinions concerning African Americans both before and after her use of the units. At the outset she recorded that her students associated African Americans with almost wholly negative traits: "In general they thought that Negroes were inferior to white persons, unclean, always fighting, dangerous, and lazy." However, as she progressed, the sentiments that students expressed began to change. As Markwell recorded, her students made comments such as, "I thought them dirty, but some are very clean"; "I thought colored people were sloppy, uneducated, now I know that they are nice"; and "I thought them different but it is only the color of their skin." Whether these responses reflect genuine growth on the part of her students, a desire to appease their teacher, or a mix of the two is almost impossible to say. However, the *Supplementary Units* at the very least provided counter-examples to the images of Black Americans that Markwell's students had clearly absorbed from the broader culture.

For Black students, the units had led to discussion not just of the Black past but of current-day structural and institutional challenges that stopped African Americans from exercising their full rights as citizens. Similarly, with Markwell's white audience, the conversations around race quickly spilled over the boundaries of historical discussion and into the present. For instance, although she does not make clear how her class arrived at the topic, Markwell notes that they engaged in conversations around race and housing. Her students initially believed that the segregation of Black people into separate areas of the city was a product of personal choice, or as one student put it, "I think Negroes just like to have their own town and don't want us to come there." As they looked more closely at the issues surrounding housing, however, the class came to the conclusion that "restricted zoning was largely responsible for the conditions in the area." Moreover, Markwell stated that as her students realized the extent of discrimination and that "certain Negroes, whom they had come to admire would not be permitted to live outside the area, their resentment flamed and they were rather vehement in their denunciation of the practice."[44] Their condemnation of housing discrimination, at least in some instances, led Markwell to put the question of integration directly to her students, asking if they would welcome Black families as neighbors in Brookfield. Of her seventy-six students, sixty-five replied positively, while a small minority believed that a Black presence might make them unsafe or otherwise "spoil the neighborhood." While not unanimous in their support for integrated housing, the students' responses show that they could move past heroes and holidays and discuss issues with immediate and personal implications. Just as important, it showed that Markwell herself was willing to engage in these types of discussions.

While Markwell was convinced that the *Supplementary Units* and the discussions that they fostered helped her students develop more open and accepting attitudes, more impactful, in her opinion, was the opportunity to create dialogue and contact across racial lines. What her students most needed, in Markwell's view, were "concrete experiences with personalities that are real," as "one person they may know is of more value than many story-book-heroes."[45] Many studies in building tolerance stressed the importance of such connections, but usually the prescriptions for action were shallow at best, never moving beyond a single invited speaker or presentation from a member of a minority group. In this case, the personal connection between Markwell and Morgan made possible a broader and longer-lasting exchange between teachers, schools, and communities, beginning with Markwell's class letter and Morgan's response to the invitation to speak in Brookfield.

Morgan accepted the request from Markwell's fifth-grade class, and although she could not visit the school before the Christmas holiday as she originally hoped, she made plans to come to Brookfield at the end of January. In preparation, Markwell's students set about purchasing her ticket, planning for the assembly, and debating what gift might be most appropriate for their honored guest. The students also diligently sought to expand their knowledge of African American history in the lead-up to Morgan's visit, forming an extracurricular club and creating a class scrapbook where they pasted pictures and detailed descriptions of notable Black figures such as George Washington Carver, Marian Anderson, and Hazel Scott, each of whom was detailed in Morgan's curriculum. As word spread throughout the school building, the event also attracted the attention of students outside of room 214, and other teachers allowed their classes to petition Markwell for invitations to the speech. As fifth-grade student Clara Donaldson wrote to Morgan on January 14, 1944:

Dear Mrs. Madeline R. Morgan,
5703 South Michigan Ave,
Chicago, 37, Illinois

We are so happy that you can come. We are inclosing rail road tickets for you and Mrs. Powell. Please let us know what time you will arrive in Brookfield so we can meet you at the train.

We decided to share the pleasure of your visit with the other children in our school. There will be about 400 of us in the auditorium.

We hope this visit will bring you as much happiness as it does us.

Sincerely Yours,
Fifth Grade, Room 214
Clara Donalson
Chairman of Arrangements[46]

When Morgan finally arrived ten days later, on the morning of January 24, 1944, she was met at the station by a small coterie of student photographers and a reception committee made up of mothers and students who presented her with flowers and ushered her to Gross Elementary. Once inside, Morgan, along with Thelma Powell, a teacher from Wendell Phillips High School who accompanied her on the trip, met with the fifth-grade class briefly, moving to the school's auditorium at 2:30 p.m. There they were treated to a color guard ceremony and the pledge of allegiance. After a short introduction by Markwell, Morgan took center stage. Her speech mixed the autobiographical, the historical, and the entertaining. She told the students about Black historical figures including educator Booker T. Washington, inventor Jan

Matzeliger, musician James Bland, and historian Carter G. Woodson, but she also spoke about her own childhood, her experiences in predominantly white schools, and the isolation and attacks she had endured in those years. She highlighted her time as a teacher, including the inequities in buildings and supplies between Black schools and white schools in the city of Chicago. After the speech, Morgan and Powell returned to Markwell's room, where the two guests took turns posing for pictures with the teacher and members of the student committee.

After the visit ended, Markwell asked her class to write their impressions, which she later transcribed. Many of the students commented on Morgan's personal bearing, describing her as "intelligent," "kind," and "distinguished."[47] This preoccupation with her personality is important because for many white students interacting with a Black woman in a position of authority was wildly outside of their day-to-day experience. Markwell noted elsewhere that the only regular contact students in her classroom had with African Americans was "on public conveyances" and that those African Americans they knew were "chiefly of the servant class." The comment suggests that Markwell's students would have been most familiar interacting with Black women as cooks or domestics, roles that demanded the women adopt a posture of deference that extended even to the young children of their white employers.[48] Simply by her presence—authoritative, well-dressed, and self-possessed—Morgan challenged the limited expectations that Markwell's students held for Black people in general and Black women in particular.

Only weeks ago, Markwell's class had discovered that Black teachers existed, and meeting Morgan was an equally eye-opening experience. One student in the welcoming committee, Patricia, captured the anxiety that surrounded this unprecedented interaction when she wrote, "When I went to the train station I was afraid. But when I was [with] Mrs. Morgan I felt sort of warm inside. . . . I seemed to know her. When she talked, I just sat and listened."[49] It is likely that many of her classmates began with similar levels of apprehension, overcoming them slowly as the day progressed. A student named Robert gave

Morgan perhaps the highest compliment he could muster, announcing, "I'd like to go to her school and I enjoyed Mrs. Morgan for a teacher. . . . I think that she would be a good teacher."[50]

Several students also wrote that meeting Morgan had helped them think more deeply about equality between racial groups. Doris Allen, for instance, foregrounded the theme of equality between the races, writing, "She made me feel that Negroes are just as good as white people." Frances Evans went further, making the connection between equality and civil rights by stating, "I don't think much about Negroes until we started studying about them and when Mrs. Morgan told about some of them I kn[e]w, that if these men and women hadn't been, this world wouldn't have been as great as it is today. Mrs. Morgan made me understand that all mankind should have the same rights."[51] For these students, Morgan's visit provided a venue to think about broader issues of racial equality.

Clearly Morgan and Powell's visit was impactful for the students of Brookfield. At the same time as historian Jonna Perrillo cautions about similar intercultural experiments in New York's schools, while such encounters were "important vehicles for the transmission of new cultural values," they were ultimately "artificial," limited by the segregation both of schooling and the broader society that students experienced on a daily basis.[52] Furthermore, by relying on these two teachers to act as representative members of their race, the assembly may also have reinforced the idea that only a few exceptional African Americans, those who measured up to or met the standards of the white world, were worthy of respect. Some students responded in ways that seemed to separate Morgan from the "Negro" race as a whole. Peggy Hall, for instance, wrote, "When she was talking I was listening so hard I forgot that she was a Negro." Echoing this language, Harold Kramer wrote, "I liked the speech very much. I never liked a Negro so much in my whole life. To Mrs. Morgan it does not matter whether she is a Negro or not and it does not matter to me either. When we walked into the room, I did not know which was which." While their assessments of Morgan were overwhelmingly positive, these reactions show that a single experience, no matter how engaging or interesting, was insufficient to change deeply held racial biases. A student named John captured this tension when he responded, "I t[h]ink both Mrs. Morgan and Mrs. Powell are very fine people," before adding, "If all Negroes were like them, what a world this would be."[53]

If some students saw Morgan as an exception, Markwell found adults whose thinking was similar. In a 1944 letter to a colleague at textbook publishing company Houghton Mifflin, for example, she remarked:

> The question I am most frequently asked is "Don't you think she is an exceptional Negro?" I might have thought so, myself, but I have met so many, who, I should have to say rank right along with her, that I should not say that. However, I am yet of the same opinion that I have held since my first conversation with her. She is an exceptional teacher as is also her philosophy of education. She is outstanding among any of us—she has to outrank us, you know, to attain the place she holds.[54]

Markwell's comment illustrates her growing belief in the equal capacity and commitment of the Black educators she met through experiences with the Urban League, NAACP, and various women's clubs Morgan introduced her to. It also shows her recognition of the systemic and institutional hurdles Black educators faced and the additional facility and skill often demanded of them.

In the end, Morgan's visit to Brookfield alone could not radically alter the attitudes of Brookfield's white youth. It could, however, open a door to continued contact and exchange, and Morgan and Markwell soon found ways to build on their momentum. The junior council for social studies at Gross School, working "under the direction of Ms. Markwell and Mrs. Morgan, a Negro teacher belonging to the Illinois Council of the Social Studies," as one local paper described, carried out a consistent plan of cultural exchanges throughout the spring of 1944.[55] Mrs. Powell of Wendell Phillips High School, who had accompanied Morgan on her initial trip to Brookfield, and La-vinia Evans, another Black teacher from Hartigan Elementary, who also became members of the ICSS committee, were key in this pro-cess. Morgan, Evans, Powell, and Markwell came to rely on each other for resources and opportunities for student engagement. In addition to written correspondence, these teachers planned a number of field trips and school visits, with Markwell's students inviting a group from Hartigan to Brookfield, and students from Gross Elementary traveling into the city to visit the Hall Branch Library, among other destina-tions on the South Side. Additional speakers also visited Brookfield, including Noma Jensen of the Chicago NAACP. Markwell recorded examples of these trips and projects:

We invited the children from Hartigan school to visit us and were invited to attend their commencement exercises.

We wrote letters to teachers in Negro schools, asking their pupils for information on Dorie Miller [a hero of the Pearl Harbor at-tack], when our library could not furnish it.

We visited [the] Hall Branch Library.

During open house, we had our Negro scrapbooks on display and pictures of our guest speaker [Morgan] on our bulletin board. Many parents asked, "Is she the colored teacher who talked to the children? J_____ has told us so much about her."[56]

The Black teachers who participated in the ICSS found the op-portunity for exchange and personal contact valuable, a way to decon-struct their students' geographical and cultural boundaries. As Evans wrote: "Of course the *Supplementary Units* are an integral part of the curriculum of the Chicago Schools. I am also planning to take our Student Council Members to Brookfield to see the Eighth Grade play 'Penrod.' . . . The trip will give our children a chance to see other neighborhoods as well as learning more about the city in which they live."[57] Markwell and Evans's comments show the way in which the *Supplementary Units* became a basis not just for classroom lessons but for social interaction and exchange, a major achievement in a city where restrictive covenants, redlining, youth gangs, and white neighborhood associations limited the potential for interracial contact of any kind.

"A Prominent Place in the Curriculum of Both Our Colored and White Schools": Assessing the Supplementary Units' *Impact*

Markwell and Morgan's efforts continued throughout the war years. Morgan was an active part of the ICSS, speaking at committee meetings in various parts of the state, writing for the organization's publication, the *Councilor,* and eventually taking up the chairmanship of the Interracial Relations Committee. Markwell, for her part, remained an enthusiastic and supportive ally. In a 1944 editorial in the *Chicago Defender,* Markwell outlined what she believed were "two of the important paths" to interracial understanding.[58] The first was "an educational program in which Negro achievement will be given a prominent place in the curriculum of both our colored and white schools." This pedagogical change would provide a firmer foundation for the second element, the development of interaction or "personal friendship" between individuals of different races. Markwell insisted that, in the end, "It is not the great Dr. Julian or Miss Anderson whom my pupils may come to know and love" but instead "people whom they may come to know personally as they have Mrs. Morgan." This two-pronged solution, in which the school curriculum served to break down barriers and prepare students for contact and communication, was just what Morgan had in mind when she began her work on the *Supplementary Units.*

Grace Markwell's belief in Morgan and her work was effusive. "I am convinced," she wrote in the conclusion of a report to the ICSS Interracial Relations Committee, "that consistent use of such materials in the schools, would, in one generation, erase the colorline from the Blackboards of America."[59] Markwell's penchant for hyperbolic language aside, Morgan's work did succeed in many ways. It offered Black students a powerful sense of racial pride and national belonging critically absent from their school experiences. It also created new spaces for white students to gain knowledge of African American achievements and engage in discussions that would never have taken place otherwise. When Black students used history to argue that they still did not have access to the rights to which they were entitled, or when white students debated housing discrimination and segregation, young people were applying what they had learned to critique present-day problems. Additionally, when utilized by committed teachers like Morgan, Evans, Markwell, and Powell, the units fostered interracial contact and cooperation between students and educators at various schools. These outcomes deserve recognition, and they amounted to a real strategy for beginning to erase the color line. However, the postwar years would see Morgan, Markwell, and others struggle to secure and expand the place of Black history and culture in the curriculum as the dedication to wartime interculturalism waned and new priorities emerged within Chicago's and the nation's schools.

CHAPTER 6

"THIS CRUCIAL WAR FOR DEMOCRACY"

Madeline Morgan and Intercultural Education in the Postwar World, 1945–1950

*T*HURSDAY, SEPTEMBER 27, 1945—Just a month after Japan's surrender spelled victory for the Allied forces and brought the Second World War to a close, new battle lines were being drawn in the city of Chicago. That morning, two hundred white students at Englewood High School, Madeline Morgan's alma mater on the city's South Side, congregated in front of the school before 9:00 a.m. and "did not enter when the bell for classes rang." By the next morning, they had been joined by hundreds more, as "some 880 absences were recorded, out of a possible 3300 students." Police squads, called to the scene to quell the unrest, proved ineffective, and by the start of the next week, white students at nearby Calumet and Morgan Park High Schools engaged in similar activity. In each case, the demands of those who participated in these "anti-Negro strikes" were clear: to maintain the institution of racial segregation by the removal of their Black peers from the buildings.[1]

The Chicago Board of Education insisted that the impetus for the strikes had come from outside the city, pointing to similar strikes at Froebel High School in Gary, Indiana, earlier that year as the "source of the infection." However, in both Chicago and Gary, new waves of

Black migration during the war years had led to postwar clashes over jobs, housing, and schools. Increasingly, there were confrontations between Black students and parents fighting for equal opportunity and access and whites who desperately sought to maintain segregated and unequal conditions. These anti-Black school strikes of the late 1940s point to a shift from fleeting wartime pluralism to postwar prejudice. The strikes also represent the difficulty, despite the efforts of liberal and progressive educators, of removing racism and intolerance from Chicago's schoolrooms. The student strikers may have initially learned hatred at home, but they found it reinforced in the classroom. As the *Defender* commented: "Why is it that democracy taught in classes has not outweighed demagogy and prejudice taught at home? One answer is that democracy is not taught within the average American school. . . . It has long been apparent that an American education does not destroy prejudice with scientific facts but cherishes it with pseudo-scientific myths."[2] The ironic result, in the *Defender's* estimation, was that "fascist seeds" were being sown in the minds of white youth at home even as "their fathers and brothers fought abroad to wipe it out." The *Defender* continued, "If we are to win this crucial war for democracy and human equality, factual, frank discussions of color and democracy must be a definite part of every school curricula. If fascism is to be rooted out of America, the digging must be done in the schoolrooms."

As the postwar era began, Morgan and other liberal educators turned their attention to this next "crucial war"—the fight to challenge prejudice and recognize Black humanity in the worsening racial climate of the late 1940s. Their efforts at postwar interculturalism, however, were increasingly met with apathy and resistance by white teachers, policy makers, and politicians. With the war over and the threat to national priorities removed, the push for tolerance education largely ebbed, as "pressure to implement prejudice reduction programs began to subside."[3] Even as a small contingent of teachers, academics, and activists held on to the promise of intercultural education, the movement largely receded from view by 1950. In Chicago, intercultural education was reduced to a human relations paradigm that traded simple "friendliness" or "getting along" for the more far-reaching goals of social equality and prejudice reduction that Morgan and others fought for.

"A Chronic Source of Racial Tensions": Wartime Migration and Postwar Violence in Chicago

The context in which Morgan and her allies pursued intercultural education in the postwar period was defined by marked reactions to major demographic shifts. The war brought increased migration and a population boom to the city. A major part of this increase came from Black migrants from the South. Between 1940 and 1944 alone, sixty thousand Black residents arrived in Chicago.[4] At the same time, city official's refusal to provide for the rapidly increasing demands on housing and city services, continuing residential segregation, and the return of servicemen at the end of the war led to an exacerbated postwar housing crisis. As the Mayor's Committee on Race Relations explained, the city had "not even approached keeping abreast with the housing needs of its Negro citizens."[5] Black residents, geographically confined to the city's already overcrowded South and West Sides, were forced to pay inflated prices and subjected to cramped, unsanitary, and often unsafe conditions. Many times, these inequities proved deadly, as multiple dilapidated structures caught fire, killing or maiming scores of residents throughout the late 1940s and early 1950s.[6]

With little new housing stock available, increasing numbers of Black families were forced to the edges of neighborhoods that had long been exclusively white. As Black families moved into previously white enclaves, however, they risked mob attack, arson, firebombing, and other forms of racial terrorism. The result was "an era of hidden violence," manifested in small-scale attacks and housing riots throughout Chicago and its close suburbs, from Englewood to Fernwood, South Deering to Cicero.[7] Ultimately, these conflicts over housing would reshape the city itself, as whites increasingly fled to outlying areas, aided by policies at both the federal and state levels, including highway creation, low-interest mortgages, and subsidized construction of new suburbs, which eased their exodus. However, in the 1940s and early 1950s, this white flight was still in the offing, and instead white Chicagoans used any means, legal or otherwise, to stop Black encroachment on what they considered their neighborhoods, and increasingly their schools as well.

The dynamics of racial segregation, and the overcrowding and lack of resources it perpetuated, were as visible in the city's schools as they were in its housing market. The mayor's commission noted that even before the war the "mounting, gross inadequacy of facilities and provisions for education" in Black schools had been "a chronic source of racial tensions." Now, however, Black students faced increased burdens; many schools were required to operate on double shifts or increase class sizes to unmanageable numbers in attempts to accommodate rapidly rising enrollments. Of the thirty-one elementary schools serving a high proportion of Black students in 1944, "None of the 31 schools had less than 36.2 pupils per teacher in September 1943; only 12 had less than 40 pupils per teacher; one had 47 pupils per teacher, and one had 49." Although the mayor's commission advocated for an intensive program of new school construction to ameliorate conditions, it admitted that "as long as Negroes in Chicago are artificially limited to living in restricted areas, it will be near to impossible to provide them with equal public facilities."[8]

Many whites fought viciously to maintain segregation in housing, and they were just as dedicated to maintaining segregated schools. The first resort of white parents whose resources allowed was simply to withdraw their pupils from schools that showed any sign of racial change. The extent to which white parents defended this prerogative was revealed when Superintendent Johnson, whose support had been critical to Morgan's ability to create her curriculum, attempted to abolish transfers in the fall of 1944 and require all students to attend schools in their designated areas. The announcement unleashed a wave of vocal criticism, street-level protests, attacks in the press, and threats of legal action from white parents fearful that their children would be forced to attend schools with increasing numbers of Black students. As the *Defender* wryly observed: "On the surface, seemingly, there should be no objection to this order, should there? However, when we prod into the situation, we find that this transfer system has been operated for a favored few and these are the ones who are causing all the turmoil. The lack of Negro parents and Negro students at these demonstrations was not accidental. Negroes had no ax to grind."[9]

The controversy reached a dangerous new pitch on September 22, 1944, when Superintendent Johnson's home and family were attacked. That night, as his eight-year-old daughter Patricia lay in bed, and while he and his wife Ellen visited with neighbors on the upper floor of the house they shared, an explosion ripped through the Johnson home, shattering windows in a two-block radius, tearing a hole in a rear wall of the apartment, and blowing a back door off its hinges. The sheer amount of explosives used, four sticks of high-grade dynamite, and the placement of the charges suggested to authorities that the attackers had prior knowledge of explosives. In response, Johnson's home, along with that of board of education president James B. McCahey, was placed under the protection of armed police, and for a short period both men were forced into hiding. The *New York Times* drew a direct line between the attack and the ongoing transfer controversy, reporting that "the bombing was the outcome of a wrangle over a ruling by which Dr. Johnson abolished the school transfer system."[10] Although Johnson and his wife escaped with only minor injuries, and his daughter emerged miraculously unhurt through the hail of broken glass that fell on her bed as she slept, Johnson had been sent a clear message. He retreated from his stand on the transfer issue. Two years later he was removed as superintendent altogether, part of a wave of white reactionary politics that would also see Mayor Ed Kelly voted out of office.[11]

White youth could be equally violent in their attempts to maintain segregation. The late 1940s saw repeated clashes between Black and white teens and young adults, most times along the racial boundaries that cut, invisible but no less real or inviolable, through the city and its public spaces, from parks to schools, sports fields to roller rinks. In 1946, for instance, the Race Relations Committee observed that "of the 19 incidents of interracial friction reported where the participants were identified, juveniles or young men were involved in 13. In 11 out of 17 attacks on individuals, juveniles and young men participated. In two cases of attacks on property, where apprehensions were made, those arrested were juveniles or very young men."[12] In response to the growing pattern of violence, the Race Relations Committee urged the Chicago police to look at these attacks "not as simple altercations between two individuals, or as simple acts of violence committed by individuals, but as premeditated, and with social consequences affecting the peace of the entire community."

In this context of growing violence against Black youth, interracial organizations such as Bishop Sheil's CYO (Catholic Youth Organization), which Morgan had worked closely with, began to falter and collapse. Young white boys and girls, who only years before participated in interracial sporting matches with Black athletes from other parishes, now "attacked African Americans as they attempted to integrate the neighborhoods of Englewood and Park Manor."[13] In this environment of surging white hostility, the commitment to pluralism shown by some during the late 1930s and 1940s was lost, and the "window of opportunity" opened to interracialists by the Depression and the war years began to close.[14]

Black educators and their allies attempted to halt this erosion of wartime progress. History teacher Samuel Stratton, an active force in the DuSable History Club and chairman of the Committee for Improving Human Relations, who became Morgan's second husband in 1946, made this objective clear in an article for the Citizens Schools Committee marking the celebration of Negro History Week. Stratton wrote that the "postwar outrages against democracy, such as have occurred in many parts of the country, including Chicago," made the ASNLH's chosen theme, "Democracy Only Possible Through Brotherhood," an "acutely appropriate" one for that year.[15] Revealing the intimately connected nature of segregation and violence in housing and schooling, and the hope that many Black educators and white allies still placed in education, he remarked,

> Student strikes protesting against the presence of Negro youth in several of our public high schools; adults resorting to the torch and terror to keep Negroes from leaving unbearable ghettos in which they have been kept by the almost universal rule of restrictive covenants; and the open mob action of the Airport Housing Project when two Negro World War II veterans tried to take their families to live in the federally financed housing project, point to the urgency of providing white Americans with information concerning the patriotic and constructive part played by Negroes in the establishment and growth of our city and our nation.

Stratton argued that one of the major barriers to successful racial integration was that Black people were presented "always as a problem to be analyzed and solved and not as a human being to be understood and appreciated as a brother in the human family." Like Morgan, he believed that communicating the "heroic struggle" of Black Americans through the schools was a key part of combating the models of Black pathology that usually framed discussions of race.[16]

"Idealism in Words, Bigotry in Action": Chicago's Schools Abandon Interculturalism

As intercultural educators in Chicago and elsewhere turned their efforts toward stemming the tide of postwar racial violence and prejudice, Morgan participated in a broad range of projects during the late 1940s. Yet while she remained active in the struggle to expand the reach of Black history in the schools and committed to the use of intercultural education as a vehicle for this work, the momentum of such efforts began to flag.

As the war neared its conclusion, there is solid evidence that Morgan's *Supplementary Units*, which debuted in 1942, were still being hailed as effective and impactful. Throughout the mid-1940s, Morgan continued to receive numerous requests from white and Black educators, for both her work and her presence as an expert on race relations. A January 1945 letter from Dr. George W. Bowles, member of an interracial commission in York, Pennsylvania, notes that Morgan's curriculum was still being sought out and recommended by recognized leaders in the field of Black education. Bowles writes that he "recently had a personal conversation with Dr. Carter G. Woodson, in regard to the introduction of Negro History into the elementary and higher grades of the school system of this city. He advised me to communicate with you and request a copy of the pamphlet, 'Supplementary Units for the Course of Instruction in Social Studies.'"[17] Bess Periman, a white sixth-grade teacher in Little Rock, Arkansas, wrote to express her "earnest desire to give my school children some kind of training which would lessen their prejudice towards the Negro race and make them more tolerant."[18] Although she admitted that her students' lack of prior work along these lines meant that she "might need to start with simpler material than you use in the sixth grade in Chicago," she nevertheless enthusiastically sought "any help" Morgan might be able to give. Closer to home, Drusilla McCormick, principal of a racially mixed school in Rock Island, Illinois, wrote with a request to use the *Supplementary Units* with her students. McCormick, who had heard of Morgan through the *Elementary English Review*, reflected the convictions of many white intercultural educators when she stated, "I firmly believe the Negro must be given a fair chance, I have been doing all in my power to develop a spirit of tolerance and understanding."[19] As such, she was convinced that "the material compiled by Miss Morgan and Mrs. King would be a great help."

In addition to the requests for her materials from classroom teachers and school administrators, Morgan also continued to be sought out by organizations committed to advancing the work of spreading Black history and interculturalism. In 1947, for example, the National Council of Negro Women (NCNW) named her as one of twelve women of the year for her "work in the field of intercultural education."[20] It was an honor she shared that year with political figures

Vijaya Lakshmi Pandit and Helen Mills Scarborough, businesswoman Sara Spencer, educators Artemisia Bowden, and entertainers Marian Anderson, among others. As NCNW president Mary McLeod Bethune, the influential educator and school founder, wrote to Morgan, the award was the result of "a nation-wide popular poll" with nominees chosen based on "their distinguished achievements."[21] The NCNW award showed that Morgan was still very much part of a national conversation about race relations and education.

However, even as Morgan continued to press forward, there was evidence that the inroads she hoped to make were meeting with increased resistance. Morgan did not often publicly acknowledge pushback, perhaps feeling that such admissions were self-defeating. It is clear from other sources, however, that even though her curriculum was taken up by a number of liberal and progressive educators in the city, the Chicago Public Schools' administration had refused to expand on Morgan's work or ensure that all teachers adopted it. The reports of the Mayor's Committee on Race Relations reveal this tension. In response to the school strikes held by segregationist students and mounting violence between Black and white youths, the committee urged expanded educational offerings aimed at building intercultural appreciation. One reason for these calls, the committee noted, was that potentially transformative efforts like Morgan's had been cordoned off and continued to be seen as asides or additions to the main curriculum:

> The Chicago Board of Education has developed materials and projects to foster intergroup understanding. This phase of the curriculum is presented as part of special programs and in supplementary units of instruction. Although some of the materials developed in Chicago have received national recognition, the present program does not really come to grips with the problem of developing interracial and intergroup understanding in the schools. This becomes apparent at times of interracial or intergroup conflicts in the schools. At such times, the fine idealism

which is contained in the special project is forgotten; the pupils are not even conscious of the inconsistency between this idealism in words and bigotry in action.[22]

The committee's remarks point to the reality that projects aimed at building intercultural knowledge and understanding could only go so far when they were presented as additional or supplemental. Although the committee called to expand on Morgan's materials, and to make them "required as part of the regular curriculum," they worried that at present the *Supplementary Units* were "optional as far as the teachers' using it is concerned." As historian Cherry McGee Banks and others have argued about such programs nationally, intercultural education "never fully permeated the schools and teacher resistance . . . was frequently tolerated."[23] In Chicago, this meant that Morgan never received the kind of backing that would have made her work part of the standard curriculum.

Perhaps because she sensed the window narrowing, both for her own efforts and for intercultural education more broadly, Morgan and her allies turned from the schools to the statehouse to concretize the gains of the war years. Working with Black state representatives Corneal Davis and Fred J. Smith, Morgan and others, including Grace Markwell, the ICSS, and Samuel Stratton, brought a bill to the floor of the Illinois House of Representatives that sought to mandate the teaching of Black history in schools throughout the state. Introduced by Smith and Davis on March 13, 1945, House Bill 251 read:

Sec. 27–23. History of the negro race shall be taught in all public schools and in all other educational institutions in this State, supported or maintained, in whole or in part, by public funds. No pupil shall be graduated from the eighth grade of any public school unless he has received such instruction in the history of the negro race and gives evidence of having a comprehensive knowledge thereof.[24]

In supporting the proposal, Davis repeated Morgan's refrain that the acknowledgment of Black history was crucial both as a means of increasing Black pride and for garnering wider support for Black rights. Davis declared that "a race is respected in proportion to its known accomplishments" and that "this bill, if passed, will bring all Americans a fuller understanding and appreciation of the Negro's role to establish our nation and to preserve it."[25] Representative Smith added, "The history of the Negro presents to us a theme of profound study, it is as worthy of perusal as that of any other group." Although Davis and Smith rehearsed arguments Morgan and her allies had made consistently throughout the late 1930s and 1940s, the legislation itself represented an evolution in thought and tactics. Morgan's experiences had convinced her that the adoption of Black history was insufficient to ensure it became a functioning part of the curriculum for all students. More than promises, pledges, or pronouncements of support, the legislation she and Davis proposed laid out clear goals and set up a system of accountability under which evidence of a minimum knowledge of Black history would be required for graduation and promotion for all students. This would ensure that teachers throughout the state, both Black and white, would be pushed to incorporate the material meaningfully into their own curricula.

The House Committee on Education met on April 24, 1945, to discuss the proposed amendment to the school code. Both Stratton and Morgan made their way two hundred miles south from Chicago to the state capital of Springfield to be on hand. That both educators' names are misspelled in the House records, hers as "Mrs. Madelaine Marvin—History teacher in Chicago" and his as "Samuel Scratton," reflected the apathy with which they were most likely greeted, but their presence in support of the bill attests to the commitment of Black educators to see the legislation passed. While no record exists of the speeches they gave, it is probable that Morgan included her work on the *Supplementary Units* and their reception in the city of Chicago, throughout the state, and nationwide in her remarks.

If Morgan, Stratton, Davis, and Smith knew the radical potential of such legislation, then its intended impact was equally clear to the lawmakers who made up the House Committee on Education. During discussion of the bill, objections were made by Representatives Skyles and Teigland, resulting in a series of changes to the original wording of the legislation. The first simply erased lines five through eight of the Davis/Smith bill. The second altered the word "shall" to "may," thus changing the inclusion of Black history from a directive to a choice, much as the *Supplementary Units* had been framed in Chicago. The revised bill read:

> Section 27–23. History of the negro race may be taught in all public schools and in all other educational institutions in this State supported or maintained, in whole or in part, by public funds.[26]

In this altered form, House Bill 251 passed through the House Committee on Education and made its way to the full House and then the Senate, where it was passed into law. What would have initially been an active requirement to teach Black history, however, had been reduced to a simple suggestion. Davis, sending a copy of the finalized wording of the bill, pointed out the disappointing changes to Morgan. He circled the word "may" and wrote beside it two short words: "Remember this."

"Intercultural Education Should Rarely Be Stressed Directly": *Herold Hunt and the Diminishment of Intercultural Education*

As the late 1940s gave way to the early 1950s, Morgan continued to see Black history kept at the margins. After the ouster of William Johnson from the superintendency in 1946, Herold Hunt, a career bureaucrat and administrator, was chosen to lead Chicago Public Schools. The Black community pressured the new superintendent and his board of education to complete what his predecessor had failed to accomplish and make Morgan's work a part of the official curriculum for all schools. As one editorialist remarked, this was a moment in which the schools could take a step to "perpetuate democracy and make it a fact rather than a sham" by teaching "the students of all races to what extent the American Negro has participated in the development of America." The material was there, "contained in Madeline Morgan Stratton's prescribed courses of study," which had been "highly praised and recommended for all of the city schools by former Superintendent Johnson." The editorial closed by insisting that "the new School Board and its superintendent would be doing an invaluable service to the entire city by approving these courses of study for use throughout the entire school system." Instead, however, despite this passionate support, the *Supplementary Units* remained where they had been left at the end of Johnson's tenure as superintendent, valued and used by a handful of teachers but unrecognized by the majority.[27]

Hunt, although he embraced intercultural education in theory, failed to strongly support it in action. Initially the new superintendent preserved several efforts at intercultural education, including the *Supplementary Units* and the monthly Americanism Bulletins that had been sent to schools throughout the war years. He also introduced new initiatives such as the creation of an official Bureau of Human Relations within the district and offered summer institutes and teacher trainings through the University of Chicago's Committee on Education, Training, and Research in Race Relations; additionally he brought the Youthbuilders, a program begun in New York, to several Chicago elementary schools. However, this flurry of activity amounted to little, as the measures were implemented only at the margins of the school system and remained voluntary in nature, never upsetting or upending the preferences of the system's majority-white teaching force. Moreover, during Hunt's tenure from 1947 to 1953, intercultural relations became synonymous with human relations, a paradigm in which the unique cultures and histories that Morgan and others had seen as strengths to be learned, celebrated, and shared were instead flattened and deemphasized.

An article from Hunt published in December 1949 made his indifference toward requiring teaching about race clear. Teachers and administrators were instructed, in a deeply ironic passage that presaged modern arguments for colorblindness, to actively avoid discussions of racial, ethnic, and cultural difference because "intercultural relations are more effectively administered by the guidance of pupils in the positive activities of harmonious living than by stressing intergroup differences and issues."[28] Moreover, such discussions should not take up an inordinate amount of the time or resources of classroom instruction, as "no aspect of intercultural relations should be permitted to distort or disturb a balanced educational program and its administration." The article also suggests that teachers should be on guard lest students use claims of racial prejudice as excuses for their own inability. According to Hunt, "Pupils should not be permitted to ascribe hardships that a pupil might normally encounter to prejudice against his group. He must be guided to the realization that 'to be able to take it' is also a part of democratic living." Finally, Hunt, in this article and elsewhere, presented racial prejudice as fundamentally outside of the school's control, as students "acquired biases and prejudices from parents and other elders" and "consequently, intercultural problems connected with the schools invariably have their origin in the community." Hunt was correct that the problem of prejudice extended far beyond the walls of the school building, yet in framing the matter as "essentially a community rather than exclusively a school issue," the superintendent also created room to absolve the school system of the very real role it played in maintaining and perpetuating racism through pupil assignment patterns, staffing, discipline, and curricula. His contention made schools bystanders to racial prejudice and avoided their obligation to take a leading role in addressing it, beginning within their own systems and structures.

Hunt's insistence that "intercultural education should rarely be stressed *directly* [emphasis original] in work with pupils, nor should attention be drawn to either the shortcomings or advantages of any particular group," was the opposite of Morgan's approach, which relied on explicit attention to the cultures and histories of groups that had been marginalized.[29] Instead, under Hunt, teachers were encouraged to concentrate on individual actors and their attitudes, with only minimal historical or social context. The results of this shift—"thin and surface level" and "culturally shallow and ineffectually bland"—were not what Morgan had pursued during the war years.[30] Instead, she had sought to explicitly teach students about the rich histories of the various groups that made up their city and nation, in hopes of enacting deeper change and sparking larger conversations.

Despite the abdication of those goals under Superintendent Hunt, Morgan herself continued to actively engage in the work. She led the Youthbuilders club at Emerson and attended summer institutes at the University of Chicago, where she led sessions and helped craft units for literature classrooms to put alongside her earlier social studies work. She continued to write, travel, and speak on issues of intercultural relations and Black history. Although her work would never again have the reach and audience it commanded during the war years, she was undeterred, remaining steadfast in her faith in education for the social good, and pragmatic in her willingness to use every available opportunity to advance her agenda.

As the nation turned from its intercultural moment, curricular experiments like Morgan's received diminished attention. The onset of the Cold War added to this trend, as conservative politicians and parents saw the creeping specter of communism in even the most mildly left-of-center reforms. Eventually even Superintendent Hunt fell victim to this fervor, accused of allowing communist influences in the schools and later removed from office. His replacement, the far more conservative Benjamin C. Willis, would be one of the most infamous and contentious superintendents in Chicago's history, a hard-nosed and tyrannical force who defended the prerogatives of white parents unremittingly over Black demands for justice and used the rhetoric of neighborhood schooling to keep Chicago segregated and unequal. Morgan weathered each of these changing regimes in turn, and although her wartime efforts proved impermanent, her presence as an educator and activist continued for decades.

EPILOGUE

IN 1965, just three years before she left the public schools, Madeline Morgan, by then Madeline Stratton, retired from the Chicago Public Schools. Her career encompassed teaching roles at Emerson, Drake, Dixon, and A. O. Sexton Elementary Schools, in addition to her work on special assignments for the Bureau of Curriculum. Even in retirement, she would continue to press for social change through education. In 1965, just four years before she left the public schools, she published a textbook, *Negroes Who Helped Build America*, a collection of biographical entries like those that made up large parts of her *Supplementary Units*. A second book, *Strides Forward: Afro-American Biographies*, followed in 1973.[1] She also continued to speak, both locally and nationally, and took active part in civil rights organizing, including with the Urban League and NAACP. Never wholly abandoning the classroom, she trained new generations of educators through lecturer positions at local colleges, including Governors State University and Chicago State University. Finally, she continued to promote Black history through the ASNLH, the organization that had given so much to her early career.

The *Supplementary Units* fell out of use after the late 1940s. Without the unifying force of an external crisis, and facing the fractious racial politics of the postwar period, the leadership of Chicago's public schools diluted and abandoned the pluralist vision Morgan and others had pursued through the classroom. To measure Morgan's success by her inability to make this work a permanent feature of the Chicago schools, however, would be to miss her larger success. By the time her curriculum fell from use in Chicago, Morgan's work had extended far beyond her own city and, as historian Ian Rocksborough Smith states, served as a blueprint "for the development of educational resources and projects elsewhere," receiving "widespread consideration among progressive educators and intellectuals throughout the country and around the world."[2] The fact that she was able to initiate, craft, and champion such a wide-reaching effort speaks to Morgan's vision and ability, as well as her place in the larger history of education and social movements.

Moreover, Morgan's demand that Black history receive a place in the school curriculum continues to hold relevance today, almost a century after she began teaching. Her conviction that the history of Black America must be acknowledged in the school curriculum anticipated the demands of civil rights workers in the 1950s, Black Power activists in the 1960s, and multiculturalists in the 1980s and 1990s. More recently, the global protest movement catalyzed by the killing of George Floyd and the onset of the global COVID-19 pandemic, the impacts of which have been felt disproportionately in Black and Brown communities, have fueled reawakened calls for racial justice both in society at large and in schools. A new generation of teachers, scholars, and activists are reimagining education in ways that fundamentally seek to address the unequal funding, inadequate resources, disproportionate discipline, and inaccurate and uninspired curricula meted out primarily to Black and low-income students. Central to this movement is the effort to confront and challenge mainstream history and social studies curricula that continue to depict Black Americans in demeaning and inaccurate ways. As the authors of *Teaching for Black Lives* make clear, the psychological and physical violence perpetrated against Black youth in schools is tied inextricably to a curriculum that "fails to respect young Black people as intellectuals, and ignores their cultures, communities, and concerns."[3]

The need for historical narratives that center the Black experience has led schools and school districts to reconsider their current teaching and look to new initiatives. There is incredible energy in the current moment, as there was during the intercultural education movement of the 1930s and 1940s. Organizations like the Southern Poverty Law Center's Learning for Justice project, the Stanford History Education Group (SHEG), the Zinn Education Project, and Facing History and Ourselves have each launched efforts to deal explicitly with the history of peoples of African descent. The College Board and its Advanced Placement program have worked with the African Diaspora Consortium to pilot a capstone course with content focused on the connections between African descended peoples in different parts of the world, and are working toward the creation of an AP African American history course, the first such effort in its seventy-year history.[4] The Black Education Research Collective at Teachers College, Columbia University, is spearheading the creation of "a citywide K–12 Black studies curriculum" for the New York City public schools.[5] Perhaps most well-known, the *New York Times*, partnering with the Pulitzer Foundation, has expanded its 1619 Project, which explores the legacies of slavery on the nation's past and future, and is creating resources that include reading guides, lesson plans, podcasts, and other curricular tools for schools and school districts. Such efforts are sorely needed because, as journalist Nikita Stewart writes, most schools still teach history through "outdated textbooks that promote long held, errant views," leaving students with a "poor understanding of how slavery shaped our country" and "unable to recognize the powerful and lasting effects it has had."[6]

As educators attempt to transform how Black history is taught and learned, there is much to gain from the historical example offered by Madeline Morgan. Corneal Davis's instruction to Morgan to "remember this" could be equally applied to modern educators, who should be mindful of both the successes and the limitations of Morgan's work.[7] One lesson that Morgan's experience highlights for the present is the role played by Black teachers in independently developing counternarratives and reframing the curriculum. Unable to rely on the insufficient material given to her by the Chicago Public Schools, Morgan instead turned to Black-led libraries, teachers' groups, sororities, and scholarly associations, bringing what she found there to her teaching. Many Black educators continue to do the same today. Their experiences should be recognized and made central to conversations about how Black histories and perspectives can best be lifted up and given space in current social studies curricula.

Another lesson that emerges from Morgan's story is the recognition that curricular change is often brought about by what Derrick Bell first articulated as interest convergence. Changes to the curriculum often occur in political and social windows when (largely white) politicians and policy makers feel that their interests and the demands of racial justice advocates align. Superintendent William H. Johnson exemplified this reality when he adopted Morgan's *Supplementary Units*, noting that "self-preservation exacts a oneness in motive and in deed."[8] On a larger scale, the proliferation of intercultural education as a movement during the Second World War was itself fueled by white American anxieties about possible fifth columns at home, and the lack of support for the war effort among disenfranchised communities, including Black Americans. While both intercultural education and the Black history movement had much deeper roots, the former stretching back to the anti-prejudice work of anthropologists and educators like Franz Boas and the latter exemplified in the work of the ASNLH that appeared decades before, the social and political backdrop of the late 1930s and early 1940s lent these movements access to a broader platform than they had previously possessed. Morgan, because of her intimate knowledge of the city and community in which she worked, was able to take hold of this national momentum and use it to bolster her own local efforts. Educators and activists today must recognize and take full advantage of the present convergence of interests to press for similar change because, as we have seen, these moments can be all too brief.

While the anxieties created by the Second World War gave Morgan a foothold in Chicago schools, it proved tenuous. By the 1950s, as the war faded from view and national priorities shifted, educators and activists struggled to hold and expand on the ground they had gained during the war years. What might have insulated the work of Morgan and others from the postwar losses they endured? This is where, I believe, a final key lesson emerges: the crucial difference between the *supplementary* and the *systemic*. While Morgan's *Supplementary Units* were a massive achievement, especially given the politics and possibilities open to her in mid-twentieth-century Chicago, their adoption was framed as an addition to the existing curriculum, not a replacement of it. The outmoded and racist texts that Morgan fought against still formed the centerpiece of the social studies curriculum, and the promises of Superintendent William H. Johnson and other officials that the *Supplementary Units* would become a mandatory part of the curriculum simply did not materialize. There was enough momentum to introduce Black history and interculturalism at the margins, but not enough to push it to the center of the curriculum.

The question of whether there is substantially more will to rethink and reshape the curriculum today remains open. There are certainly signs that this moment could yield substantive victories. In 2019, for example, Chicago Public Schools adopted the 1619 Project curriculum as part of the district's efforts to give students a more "honest accounting of our country's past."[9] The district backed words with actions, providing copies of the original *New York Times Magazine* edition of the project to all high school–level social studies teachers, along with access to other resources. However, the 1619 Project still constitutes an addition to, not a replacement of, the existing social studies curriculum, and the decision about how to use these materials, and indeed, whether to use them at all, will be left to individual schools and teachers. At the state level, the Black Caucus of the Illinois General Assembly succeeded in gaining the passage of House Bill 5851, the Inclusive American History Act, which aims to expand the breadth and depth of Black history taught throughout the state. Steps like these, building on the urgency of this historical moment, have the potential to move real and relevant histories into the heart of the curriculum. Whether these attempts succeed in the long run, however, as Morgan's work teaches us, will be determined by whether

Black history advocates and their allies use this moment to its fullest potential, and how they continue the fight when the moment fades.

ACKNOWLEDGMENTS

*W*RITING A BOOK, especially a first book, is a far larger task than any one person could complete alone, and I am lucky to have had an enormous amount of help along the way. I would like to thank my instructors and mentors at Loyola University Chicago, especially Ann Marie Ryan, Charles Tocci, and Noah Sobe. I owe a tremendous debt to Ansley Erickson and Cally Waite of Teachers College Columbia University, who offered guidance as I transformed my dissertation into a book proposal and began the journey of rewriting this story for a broader audience. My colleagues at Stanford University's Graduate School of Education have also been pivotal in this work. Conversations with David Labaree, Larry Cuban, Mitchell Stevens, Subini Annamma, Sam Wineburg, Alvin Pearman, and Farzana Saleem, among many others, were a continual source of inspiration. Just as important, the opportunity to be in community with amazing students in my survey course on the history of American education and seminar in African American education added tremendously to my thinking around this project.

To tell this story as fully as possible I have relied on hundreds of letters, oral history interviews, articles, meeting notes, lesson plans, and pieces of student work. The libraries of Loyola University Chicago, Northwestern University, Chicago State University, and the State Library of Michigan; the records of newspapers including the *Chicago Tribune* and the *Chicago Defender*; and the archives of the Chicago History Museum were among the most crucial and revisited sites of research. The HistoryMakers oral history collection allowed me to hear from Madeline Stratton Morris herself, in interviews conducted in her waning years. Most importantly, the Vivian G. Harsh Collection of the Woodson Regional Library in Chicago, where the Madeline Stratton Morris Papers are stored, became a kind of second home. I owe an incalculable amount to the archivists and staff of these institutions for making this research possible, and I hope that what emerges here reflects the careful work they have done in preserving the past for our interrogation and study.

Finally, and most importantly of all, my family has been a source of constant encouragement and understanding. My parents, Michael and Teresa Hines, my wife Erica, and my son Elijah deserve more thanks than I can possibly put into words. This book is the result of your support, and I hope more than anything to have done you proud.

NOTES

Introduction

1. Edward Butler to Madeline Morgan, November 5, 1943, Madeline Stratton Morris Papers [manuscript], 1941–1945, United States, World War II Miscellaneous Collection, Chicago History Museum.

2. Madeline Morgan, "Chicago Schools Teach Negro History," *Elementary English Review* 21, no. 3 (March 1944): 108.

3. Fletcher Wilson, "How Chicago Teaches Whites to Respect Negroes and Negroes to Respect Themselves," *PM*, September 5, 1943, 15.

4. William Johnson, Leo Herdeg, and Mary Lusson, *Supplementary Units for the Course of Instruction in Social Studies Grades 1–2–3: Negroes in American Life* (Chicago: Chicago Bureau of Curriculum, 1942), 1. Although Madeline Morgan and Bessie King authored the *Supplementary Units*, they are listed below Chicago Public Schools Superintendent Johnson, Assistant Superintendent Herdeg, and Mary Lusson, the head of the Bureau of Curriculum. Morgan and King are credited only with having "prepared" the material.

5. References to Morgan and her work appear in education histories including Alana D. Murray, *The Development of the Alternative Black Curriculum, 1890–1940: Countering the Master Narrative* (London: Palgrave Macmillan, 2018); Jarvis Givens, *Fugitive Pedagogy: Carter G. Woodson and the Art of Black Teaching* (Cambridge, MA: Harvard University Press, 2021); and Zoe Burkholder, "'Education for Citizenship in a Bi-Racial Civilization': Black Teachers and the Social Construction of Race, 1929–1954," *Journal of Social History* 46, no. 2 (2012): 335–63. Additionally, she is referenced in works dealing with public history and women's activism including Ian Rocksborough Smith, *Black Public History in Chicago: Civil Rights Activism from World War II until the Cold War* (Champaign: University of Illinois Press, 2018); Anne Meis Knupfer, *The Chicago Black Renaissance and Women's Activism* (Champaign: University of Illinois Press, 2006); and Timothy Neary, *Crossing Parish Boundaries: Race, Sports, and Catholic Youth in Chicago, 1914–1954* (Chicago: University of Chicago Press, 2016).

6. Pero G. Dagbovie, *The Early Black History Movement, Carter G. Woodson, and Lorenzo Johnston Greene* (Urbana: University of Illinois Press, 2007), 3.

7. Carter G. Woodson, "Negro History Week," *Journal of Negro History* 11, no. 2 (1926): 238.

8. James D. Anderson, "Secondary School History Textbooks and the Treatment of Black History," in *The State of Afro-American History: Past, Present, and Future*, ed. Darlene Clarke Hine (Baton Rouge: Louisiana State University Press, 1986).

9. Stuart J. Foster, "The Struggle for American Identity: Treatment of Ethnic Groups in United States History Textbooks," *History of Education Quarterly* 28, no. 3 (1999): 265.

10. Carter G. Woodson, *The Mis-Education of the Negro* (Washington, DC: Associated Publishers, 1933, 1969), 3.

11. Murray, *The Development of the Alternative Black Curriculum*, 3.

12. See LaGarrett J. King, "When Lions Write History: Black History Textbooks, African American Educators, and the Alternative Black Curriculum in Social Studies Education, 1890–1940," *Multicultural Education* 2, no. 1 (2014): 2–11; ArCasia D. James-Gallaway, "Problems and Alternatives: A Historiographical Review of Primary and Secondary Black History Curriculum, 1900–1950," in *Perspectives of Black History in Schools*, ed. LaGarrett King (Charlotte, NC: Information Age Publishing, 2020).

13. Murray, *The Development of the Alternative Black Curriculum*, 6.

14. Pero Gaglo Dagbovie, "Black Women Historians from the Late 19th Century to the Dawning of the Civil Rights Movement," *Journal of African American History* 89, no. 3 (2004): 241–61, esp. 242.

15. Dagbovie, *The Early Black History Movement*, 50.

16. Barbara Finkelstein, "Revealing Human Agency: The Uses of Biography in the Study of Educational History," in *Writing Educational Biography: Explorations in Qualitative Research*, ed. Craig Kridel (New York: Garland, 1998), 46.

17. Franklin D. Roosevelt, "February 23, 1942, Fireside Chat 20: On the Progress of the War," Miller Center, University of Virginia, https://millercenter.org/the-presidency/presidential-speeches/february-23-1942-fireside-chat-20-progress-war.

18. Dan Shiffman, "A Standard for the Wise and Honest: The 'Americans All, Immigrants All' Radio Broadcasts," *Studies in Popular Culture* 19, no. 1 (1996): 99.

19. Burkholder, "'Education for Citizenship in a Bi-Racial Civilization,'" 344.

20. Madeline Morgan, "The Intellectual Emancipation of the Negro, *The Councilor*, Jan. 1944," Madeline Stratton Morris Papers, box 2, folder 5, Vivian G. Harsh Research Collection of Afro-American History and Literature, Chicago Public Library (hereafter MSM Papers).

21. James Banks, "African American Scholarship and the Evolution of Multicultural Education," *Journal of Negro Education* 61, no. 3 (1992): 273–86. Banks, for instance, argues that the intercultural education and Black history movements "pursued their goals quite independently" (279). While this is true to some extent, such an interpretation ignores the moments of intersection between these two

movements and what they can teach us about how curricular reforms take shape, spread, and subside.

22. Namuh Brascher, "Honor School Chief for New History Course Plan," *Chicago Defender*, June 20, 1942.

23. Derrick Bell, *Silent Covenants: Brown v. Board of Education and the Unfulfilled Hopes for Racial Reform* (New York: Oxford University Press, 2004), 56. Bell argues that "even a rather cursory look at American political history suggests that in the past, the most significant political advances for blacks resulted from policies which were intended to serve, and had the effect of serving, the interests and conveniences of whites rather than remedying racial injustices against blacks."

24. Board of Education, City of Chicago, *The Chicago Public Schools in Wartime: Published as the Annual Report of the Superintendent of Schools for the School Years 1941–1942, 1942–1943* (Chicago: Board of Education, 1943), 186.

25. Manning Marable, *Living Black History: How Reimagining the African American Past Can Remake America's Racial Future* (New York: Basic Civitas Books, 2006), 37.

Chapter 1: "Knowledge Is Power Only If It Is Put Into Action"

1. Ora MacDonald to Madeline R. Morgan, January 10, 1944, Alumni Biographical Files, series 51/14, box 1576, Northwestern University Archives, Evanston, Illinois (hereafter Alumni Files).

2. Madeline Morgan to Ora McDonald, *Northwestern University Alumni News*, January 13, 1944, Alumni Files.

3. Chicago Commission on Race Relations, *The Negro in Chicago: A Study of Race Relations and a Race Riot in 1919* (Chicago: University of Chicago Press, 1922), 106.

4. "A Chicago 'Nigger' Preacher, a 'Feeder' of the 'Little Hells,' Springs Up to Hinder Our Brethren Coming North," *Chicago Defender*, July 23, 1917, 1.

5. J. R. Grossman, *Land of Hope: Chicago, Black Southerners, and the Great Migration* (Chicago: University of Chicago Press, 1989), 29.

6. "A New Accent in the Negroes Progress," *Chicago Defender*, October 29, 1910, 6.

7. Darlene Clarke Hine and John McCluskey Jr., eds., *The Black Chicago Renaissance* (Urbana: University of Illinois Press, 2012). xv. For more on the growth of Chicago's Black community during the Great Migration, see Timuel Black Jr., *Bridges of Memory: Chicago's First Wave of Black Migration* (Evanston, IL: Northwestern University Press, 2007); Adam Green, *Selling the Race: Culture, Community, and Black Chicago, 1940–1955* (Chicago: University of Chicago Press, 2007); and Davarian Baldwin, *Chicago's New Negroes: Modernity, the Great Migration, and Black Urban Life* (Chapel Hill: University of North Carolina Press, 2007).

8. Grossman, *Land of Hope*, 166. Grossman argues that white Chicagoans and their southern peers were "equally committed to white supremacy" but that "without the threat of a significant black population 'the preoccupation with the issue of race' so essential to southern culture in the early twentieth century was

unnecessary, if not irrelevant, in Chicago." This calculus, however, began to change as the Black population grew during the Great Migration.

9. Chicago Commission on Race Relations, *The Negro in Chicago*, 119.

10. Chicago Commission on Race Relations, *The Negro in Chicago*, 122.

11. Fletcher Wilson, "How Chicago Teaches Whites to Respect Negroes and Negroes to Respect Themselves," *PM*, September 5, 1943, 15.

12. Chicago Commission on Race Relations, *The Negro in Chicago*, 4.

13. W. E. B. Du Bois, *The Souls of Black Folk*, Norton Critical Edition, ed. Henry Louis Gates Jr. and Terri Hume Oliver (New York: Norton, 1999), 17.

14. Chicago Commission on Race Relations, *The Negro in Chicago*, 100–101. When new arrivals enumerated the benefits they hoped to enjoy in Chicago, education was featured prominently and consistently. Statements such as "The schools for the children, the better wages, and privileges for colored folk"; "More enjoyment; more places of attraction; better treatment; better schools for the children"; and "Privileges, freedom, industrial and educational facilities"; and "Liberty, better schools" surface numerous times in the reflections of migrants.

15. Christopher R. Reed, *Black Chicago's First Century: 1833–1900* (Columbia: University of Missouri Press, 2005), 11. The Chicago Public Schools, unlike most school systems in both the North and the South, had a tradition of integrated education that stretched back intermittently to the antebellum period. A large portion of Chicago's early settlers had come from the northeastern states, bringing with them liberal leanings and abolitionist political stances, and the resulting mix of "New England morality and municipal fiat" ensured that the city's early schools would be open to all children. While Chicago's first established school system in the 1830s followed state ordinances limiting school to white children, city ordinances in 1849 and 1851 broke with the state and opened the public schools to students regardless of race or color. By 1861, there were 212 Black students attending the city schools, and when the first high school was constructed in 1856, one of its early graduates was a Black girl named Mary E. Mann. For more on this topic, see also Mary Herrick, *The Chicago Schools: A Social and Political History* (Beverly Hills, CA: Sage, 1971).

16. Worth Kamili Hayes, *Schools of Our Own: Chicago's Golden Age of Black Private Education* (Evanston, IL: Northwestern University Press, 2020), 21.

17. Chicago Commission on Race Relations, *The Negro in Chicago*, 243.

18. Michael Homel, "The Politics of Public Education in Black Chicago, 1910–1941," *Journal of Negro Education* 45, no. 2 (1976): 182.

19. Chicago Commission on Race Relations, *The Negro in Chicago*, 242.

20. Madeline Stratton Morris, interviewed by Larry Crowe, August 28, 2003, HistoryMakers Digital Archive A2003.209, session I, tape 2, story 8. Morris talks about her favorite teachers at Farren School in Chicago.

21. Morris, Crowe interview, session I, tape 2, story 8.

22. Wilson, "How Chicago Teaches Whites to Respect Negroes and Negroes to Respect Themselves," 14.

23. Morris, Crowe interview, session I, tape 3, story 3, about her experiences of racial discrimination at Englewood High School in the 1910s.

24. Chicago Commission on Race Relations, *The Negro in Chicago*, 254.

25. "Principal Admits He Used Czarlike Power in Case of Student," *Chicago Defender*, December 22, 1923.

26. "Chicago School Advocates Southern Hates," *Chicago Defender*, January 7, 1928.

27. Wayne Au, Anthony L. Brown, and Dolores Calderon, *Reclaiming the Multicultural Roots of U.S. Curriculum: Communities of Color and Official Knowledge in Education* (New York: Teachers College Press, 2016), 117.

28. Madeline Morgan, "Chicago Public Schools Project, 1942," MSM Papers, box 2, folder 12, 1–2.

29. "Chicago School Advocates Southern Hates."

30. Morris, Crowe interview, session I, tape 3, story 4, about her trajectory to attend Chicago Teachers College.

31. William H. Watkins, "Black Curriculum Orientations: A Preliminary Inquiry," *Harvard Educational Review* 60, no. 3 (1993).

32. Karen A. Johnson, Abul Pitre, and Kenneth L. Johnson, eds., *African American Women Educators: A Critical Examination of Their Pedagogies, Educational Ideas, and Activism from the Nineteenth to the Mid-Twentieth Century* (New York: Rowman & Littlefield, 2014), xvi. There is a deep and well-developed historical literature on the teaching profession and Black women's social activism in the late nineteenth and early twentieth centuries. For other outstanding examples of this literature, see Vanessa Siddle-Walker, *Their Highest Potential: An African American School Community in the Segregated South* (Chapel Hill: University of North Carolina Press, 2007); Karen A. Johnson, *Uplifting the Women and the Race: The Educational Philosophies and Social Activism of Anna Julia Cooper and Nannie Helen Burroughs* (New York: Routledge, 2000); Sonya Ramsey, *Reading, Writing, and Segregation: A Century of Black Women Teachers in Nashville* (Urbana: University of Illinois Press, 2008). For studies of Black women's activism more broadly, see Paula J. Giddings, *When and Where I Enter: The Impact of Black Women on Race and Sex in America* (New York: Harper Collins, 1984); D. G. White, *Too Heavy a Load: Black Women in Defense of Themselves, 1894–1994* (New York: Norton, 1999).

33. Elizabeth Todd Breeland, *A Political Education: Black Politics and Education Reform in Chicago Since the 1960s* (Chapel Hill: University of North Carolina Press, 2018), 8.

34. Paula J. Giddings, *In Search of Sisterhood: Delta Sigma Theta and the Challenge of the Black Sorority Movement* (New York: Amistad, 2006) 31.

35. Edmund W. Kearny, *A History, Chicago State University, 1867–1979: Part I, A Centennial Retrospective* (Chicago: Chicago State University Foundation, 1979), 22.

36. For histories of the progressive education movement, see Lawrence Cremin, *The Transformation of the School: Progressivism in American Education, 1876–1957* (New York: Knopf, 1961); Herbert M. Kliebard, *The Struggle for the American Curriculum, 1893–1958*, 3rd ed. (New York: Routledge, 2004); David Tyack, *The One Best System: A History of American Urban Education* (Cambridge, MA: Harvard University Press, 1974); Arthur Zilversmit, *Changing Schools: Progressive Education and Practice, 1930–1960*

(Chicago: University of Chicago Press, 1993); David Labaree, "Progressivism, Schools, and Schools of Education: An American Romance," *Paedagogica Historica* 41, no. 1 (2005): 275–88; Jeffrey Mirel, "Old Educational Ideas, New American Schools: Progressivism and the Rhetoric of Educational Revolution," *Paedagogica Historica* 29 (2003): 477–97; William J. Reese, "The Origins of Progressive Education," *History of Education Quarterly* 41, no. 2 (2001): 1–24.

37. "Chicago Normal Course Announcement for 1928–1929: A Statement of the Organization and Courses of Study of the Chicago Normal College," Chicago Normal College Records, box 1, folder 2, Chicago State University, Archives and Special Collections, 23.

38. "Chicago Normal Course Announcement for 1928–1929," 24.

39. Madeline Morgan, "Chicago Public Schools Project, 1942," MSM Papers, box 2, folder 12, 1.

40. Bruce Colwell, "The Study of Education at Northwestern University, 1900–1945: Institutional Conflicts of Mission and Men" (PhD diss., Northwestern University, 1988), 216.

41. Colwell, "The Study of Education at Northwestern University," 220.

42. Harold Williamson and Payson Wild, *Northwestern University: A History, 1850–1975* (Evanston, IL: Northwestern University Press, 1976), 194.

43. Thomas D. Fallace, "The Racial and Cultural Assumptions of the Early Social Studies Educators, 1901–1922," in *Histories of Social Studies and Race*, ed. Christine Woyshner and Chara Haeussler Bohan (New York: Palgrave Macmillan, 2012); Ronald K. Goodenow, "The Progressive Educator, Race and Ethnicity During the Depression Years: An Overview," *History of Education Quarterly* 15, no. 4 (1975); LaGarrett J. King, Christopher Davis, and Anthony L. Brown, "African American History, Race, and Textbooks: An Examination of the Works of Harold O. Rugg and Carter G. Woodson," *Journal of Social Studies Research* 36, no. 4 (2012); Frank Margonis, "John Dewey's Racialized Visions of the Student and Classroom Community," *Educational Theory* 59, no. 1 (2009): 17–39.

44. Madeline Morgan, "Chicago Intergroup Workshop: Emerson School Background," MSM Papers, box 7, folder 2.

45. Carter G. Woodson, *The Mis-Education of the Negro* (Washington, DC: Associated Publishers, 1933, 1969), 192.

46. Pero G. Dagbovie, *The Early Black History Movement, Carter G. Woodson, and Lorenzo Johnston Greene* (Urbana: University of Illinois Press, 2007), 50–51.

47. "ASNLH, Annual Meetings and Anniversary Celebrations, 1935–1940," Hall Branch Papers, box 5, folder 45, Vivian G. Harsh Research Collection of Afro-American History and Literature, Chicago Public Library (hereafter Hall Branch Papers).

48. Dagbovie, *The Early Black History Movement*, 99.

49. Jarvis Givens, *Fugitive Pedagogy: Carter G. Woodson and the Art of Black Teaching* (Cambridge, MA: Harvard University Press, 2021), 82.

50. Mavis Mixon, "The Development of the Study of Negro History in Chicago," *Chicago Defender*, February 7, 1942, 15.

51. Madeline Morgan, "Chicago Public Schools Project, 1942," MSM Papers, box 2, folder 12.

52. Charlemae Rollins, "Library Work with Negroes," Hall Branch Papers, box 3, folder 30.

53. Melanie Chambliss, "A Vital Factor in the Community: Recovering the Life and Legacy of Chicago Public Librarian Vivian G. Harsh," *Journal of African American History* 106, no. 3 (2021): 417.

54. "The Historian Who Never Wrote," *Chicago Defender*, August 29, 1960.

55. Christopher R. Reed, *The Rise of Chicago's Black Metropolis, 1920–1929* (Champaign: University of Illinois Press, 2011), 52.

56. Sarah A. Anderson, "'A Place to Go': The 135th Street Branch Library and the Harlem Renaissance," *Library Quarterly: Information, Community, Policy* 73, no. 4 (2003): 386.

57. Anne Meis Knupfer, *The Chicago Black Renaissance and Women's Activism* (Champaign: University of Illinois Press, 2006), 63.

58. Gwendolyn Brooks, "For Charlemae Rollins," Hall Branch Papers, box 3, folder 14, Vivian G. Harsh Research Collection of Afro-American History and Literature, Chicago Public Library.

59. Charlemae Rollins, "Library Work with Negroes," Hall Branch Papers, box 3, folder 30,

60. Charlemae Hill Rollins, ed., *We Build Together: A Reader's Guide to Negro Life and Literature for Elementary and High School Use* (New York: National Council of Teachers of English, 1941).

61. "Phi Delta Kappa Sorority Here: Rebecca Young Heads Local Chapter," *Chicago Defender*, February 14, 1931.

62. "Phi Delta Kappa Sorors Plan Educational Confab," *Chicago Defender*, October 17, 1936.

63. "Sorors Plan for Character Week," *Chicago Defender*, June 4, 1938.

64. Dionne Danns, "Thriving in the Midst of Adversity: Educator Maudelle Brown Bousfield's Struggles in Chicago, 1920–1950," *Journal of Negro Education* 78, no. 1 (2009): 12.

65. Madeline Stratton, "Public Addresses, [Maudelle Brown Bousfield] (St. Edmund's Episcopal), 1967," MSM Papers, box 4, folder 14, 3.

66. "'Study Negro History' Says Stratton to Group," *Chicago Defender*, December 28, 1940.

67. Vernon Jarrett, "Past Is Important to Blacks' Identity," *Chicago Tribune*, February 16, 1972.

68. Madeline Morgan, "Are Negroes Intellectually Free?" MSM Papers, box 4, folder 1, 5.

69. Madeline Morgan, "Negro History and American Democracy," MSM Papers, box 4, folder 35, 1, 2.

70. Morgan, "Negro History and American Democracy," 3.

Chapter 2: "Self-Preservation Exacts a Oneness in Motive and in Deed"

1. Hugh S. Gardner, "American Negro Exposition an Inspiration to Both Races," *Pittsburgh Courier*, July 13, 1940.

2. "Await Exposition Opening," *Chicago Defender*, June 29, 1940.

3. Mabel O. Wilson, *Negro Building: Black Americans in the World of Fairs and Museums* (Los Angeles: University of California Press, 2012), 222. The American Negro Exposition was one of several emancipation expositions organized between 1910 and the 1960s in cities including Detroit, Chicago, Atlanta, and New Orleans.

4. American Negro Exposition, *American Negro Exposition, 1863–1940: Chicago Coliseum—July 4 to Sept. 2: Official Program and Guide Book* (1940), https://archive.org /details/americannegroexp00amer.

5. "Dustin' Off the News," *Chicago Defender*, July 6, 1940.

6. "President Roosevelt Opens Exhibition," *Chicago Defender*, July 13, 1940.

7. "Billikens Frolic at American Negro Exposition," *Chicago Defender*, Aug. 31, 1940.

8. Madeline Morgan, "Chicago School Curriculum Includes Negro Achievements," *Journal of Negro Education* 13, no. 1 (Winter 1944): 120.

9. Madeline Morgan, "Untitled (Cooperation on Social Studies Curriculum)," n.d., MSM Papers, box 3, folder 8, 6.

10. Morgan, "Untitled (Cooperation on Social Studies Curriculum)," n.d., MSM Papers, box 3, folder 8, 6.

11. Madeline Morgan to William H. Johnson, MSM Papers, box 6, folder 17, 1.

12. Lucius Harper, "Dustin' Off the News: It's the People Who Should Vote, 'War or No War,'" *Chicago Defender*, July 20, 1940.

13. Ethan Michaeli, *The Defender: How the Legendary Black Newspaper Changed America, from the Age of the Pullman Porters to the Age of Obama* (Boston: Houghton Mifflin Harcourt, 2016), 243.

14. Margaret Taylor Goss, "A Negro Mother Looks at the War," *Chicago Defender*, August 31, 1940.

15. "For Democracy and Unity," *Chicago Defender*, December 13, 1941.

16. "Balks Call to Arms; Cites Jim Crow: Youth Makes Issue of Army Race Policy," *Chicago Defender*, January 11, 1941.

17. "The Courier's Double V for a Double Victory Campaign Gets Country-Wide Support," *Pittsburgh Courier*, February 14, 1942. The Double V campaign, which lasted from 1942 to 1945, began in response to a letter to the editors of the *Courier* from James G. Thompson, "Should I Sacrifice to Live 'Half-American?': Suggest Double VV for Double Victory against Axis Forces and Ugly Prejudices on the Home Front," *Pittsburgh Courier*, January 31, 1942. For more on how the Second World War sparked social activism within the Black community, see Kimberley L. Phillips, *War! What Is It Good For? Black Freedom Struggles and the U.S. Military from World War II to Iraq* (Chapel Hill: University of North Carolina Press, 2012); Philip McGuire, ed., *Taps for a Jim Crow Army: Letters from Black Soldiers in World War II* (Lexington: University Press of Kentucky, 1983); Neil A. Wynn, *The African American Experience*

During World War II (New York: Rowman & Littlefield, 2010); Ronald Takaki, *Double Victory: A Multicultural History of America in World War II* (New York: Little, Brown, 2000); and Rawn James Jr., *The Double V: How Wars, Protest, and Harry Truman Desegregated America's Military* (New York: Bloomsbury Press, 2013).

18. American Negro Exposition, *American Negro Exposition* official program, 4.

19. Robert Rydell, *World of Fairs: The Century of Progress Expositions* (Chicago: University of Chicago Press, 1993), 167.

20. American Negro Exposition, *American Negro Exposition* official program, 5.

21. American Negro Exposition, *American Negro Exposition* official program, 5.

22. Robert Rydell, *World of Fairs*, 191.

23. Robert Fleeger, "Forget All Differences Until the Forces of Freedom Are Triumphant," *Journal of American Ethnic History* 27, no. 2 (2008): 62.

24. John W. Studebaker, "Teaching Tolerance a Major Problem in 1939," *Clearing House* 13, no. 5 (1939): 266.

25. John W. Studebaker, "U.S. Education Chief Outlines a Victory Program to Strengthen National Unity and Morale," *Chicago Defender*, December 19, 1942.

26. Diana Selig, *Americans All: The Cultural Gifts Movement* (Cambridge, MA: Harvard University Press, 2008), 235.

27. Rachel Davis DuBois, "Developing Sympathetic Attitudes Toward Peoples," *Journal of Educational Sociology* 9, no. 7 (1936): 389.

28. Zoe Burkholder, "From 'Wops and Dagoes and Hunkies' to 'Caucasian': Changing Racial Discourse in American Classrooms during World War II," *History of Education Quarterly* 50, no. 3 (2010): 335.

29. US Department of Interior, Office of Education, *Americans All—Immigrants All* (Washington, DC: US Department of the Interior, Office of Education, 1939), 2.

30. "New Federal Broadcast: It Will Describe Contribution of Racial Minorities," *New York Times*, September 29, 1938.

31. Dan Shiffman, "A Standard for the Wise and Honest: The 'Americans All, Immigrants All' Radio Broadcasts," *Studies in Popular Culture* 19, no. 1 (1996): 99.

32. "Americanism Wins in Radio Poll," *New York Times*, April 23, 1939.

33. "Negro History Week Should Be Wisely Observed," *Negro History Bulletin* 8, no. 5 (1945): 108.

34. "Tolerance and the Negro," *Negro History Bulletin* 7, no. 7 (1944): 168.

35. Jonna Perrillo, *Uncivil Rights: Teachers, Unions, and the Battle for School Equity* (Chicago: University of Chicago Press, 2012), 49.

36. Ambrose Caliver, "Schools in the War Effort: Negro Teachers Face Special Task in Training Men for War Work, Spreading Message of Democracy," *Chicago Defender*, December 19, 1942.

37. L. D. Reddick, "Propaganda and Prejudice," *Chicago Defender*, September 26, 1942.

38. National Association for the Advancement of Colored People, *Anti-Negro Propaganda in School Textbooks* (New York: NAACP, 1939), 6, 7, 15.

39. Albert Beckham, "Negro Children in Wartime: Negro Youth Asks Parents Why Jim Crow Exists, Fight Challenge to Their Democracy," *Chicago Defender*, December 19, 1942. For more background on Albert Beckham, see Scott L. Graves Jr., "Alfred Sidney Beckham: The First Black School Psychologist," *School Psychology International* 30, no. 1 (2009).

40. "Bishop Sheil's Speech," *Chicago Defender*, October 10, 1942; "Catholic Bishop Hits Racial Discrimination," *Chicago Defender*, October 3, 1942.

41. Timothy B. Neary, *Crossing Parish Boundaries: Race, Sports, and Catholic Youth in Chicago, 1914–1954* (Chicago: University of Chicago Press, 2016), 160–62.

42. Burkholder, "Education for Citizenship in a Bi-Racial Civilization," 345.

43. Board of Education, City of Chicago, *The Chicago Public Schools in Wartime: Published as the Annual Report of the Superintendent of Schools for the School Years 1941–1942, 1942–1943* (Chicago: Board of Education, 1943), 157, 27.

44. Madeline Morgan to Phi Delta Kappa Sorors, May 19, 1942, MSM Papers, box 9, folder 46.

45. Rollins, "Library Work with Negroes," Hall Branch Papers, box 3, folder 30.

46. Johnson et al., *Supplementary Units, Grades 1–2–3*, 5.

47. William Johnson, "William M. Johnson (Supt. of Chicago Board of Education), 1941–1945," MSM Papers, box 6, folder 17.

48. William H. Johnson, "The Negro in History Books," *Chicago Defender*, September 26, 1942.

49. Board of Education, City of Chicago, *The Chicago Public Schools in Wartime*, 186.

50. Derrick Bell, *Silent Covenants:* Brown v. Board of Education *and the Unfilled Hopes for Racial Reform* (New York: Oxford University Press, 2004), 69.

51. Bell, *Silent Covenants*, 49; see also Mary Dudziak, "Brown as a Cold War Case," *Journal of American History* 91, no. 1 (June 2004). Critical race theory (CRT) and the principle of interest convergence have been taken up powerfully and usefully by scholars of education for decades. For an early example of this work, see Gloria Ladson Billings, "What Is Critical Race Theory and What Is It Doing in a Nice Field Like Education?" *International Journal of Qualitative Studies in Education* 11, no 1 (1998).

52. Bell, *Silent Covenants*, 59.

Chapter 3: "A Worthy Piece of Work"

1. Madeline Morgan to Phi Delta Kappa Sorors, May 19, 1942, MSM Papers, box 9, folder 46.

2. Morgan to Phi Delta Kappa Sorors, May 19, 1942.

3. Morgan to Phi Delta Kappa Sorors, May 19, 1942.

4. Alana D. Murray, *The Development of the Alternative Black Curriculum, 1890–1940: Countering the Master Narrative* (London: Palgrave Macmillan, 2018), 3.

5. Murray, *The Development of the Alternative Black Curriculum*, 64.

6. Wayne Au, Anthony L. Brown, and Dolores Calderon, *Reclaiming the Multicultural Roots of U.S. Curriculum: Communities of Color and Official Knowledge in Education* (New York: Teachers College Press, 2016), 140.

7. Jeannette Eileen Jones, *In Search of Brightest Africa: Reimagining the Dark Continent in American Culture, 1884–1936* (Athens: University of Georgia Press, 2010), 3.

8. Penny M. Von Eschen, *Race Against Empire: Black Americans and Anticolonialism, 1937–1957* (Ithaca, NY: Cornell University Press, 1997), 7.

9. James H. Merriweather, *Proudly, We Can Be Africans: Black Americans and Africa, 1935 to 1961* (Chapel Hill: University of North Carolina Press, 2019), 3.

10. Freeden Blume Oeur, "The Children of the Sun: Celebrating the One Hundred Year Anniversary of *The Brownies' Book," Journal of the History of Childhood and Youth* 14, no. 3 (2021): 330. The *Brownies' Book* originally grew out of the annual children's number of the NAACP's magazine *The Crisis: A Record of the Darker Races.* The publication only ran from 1920 to 1921, but its cultural impact long outlived its short print run. See also Dianne Johnson Feelings, *The Best of the Brownies' Book* (New York: Oxford University Press, 1996).

11. Carter G. Woodson, *Negro Makers of History* (Washington, DC: Associated Publishers, 1928), 9–10.

12. Carter G. Woodson, *African Heroes and Heroines* (Washington, DC: Associated Publishers, 1939; reprint, Brattleboro, VT: Echo Point, 2015), 1.

13. Anthony L. Brown, "Counter-Memory and Race: An Examination of African American Scholars' Challenges to Early Twentieth Century K–12 Historical Discourses," *Journal of Negro Education* 97, no. 1 (2010): 60.

14. Daniel J. Beeby, *America's Roots in the Past* (Chicago: Charles Merrill, 1927), 2.

15. Beeby, *America's Roots in the Past,* 12.

16. Ruth West and Willis M. West, *The Story of Our Country* (Chicago: Allyn & Bacon, 1935), v.

17. Brown, "Counter-Memory and Race," 60.

18. William Johnson, Leo Herdeg, and Mary Lusson, *Supplementary Units for the Course of Instruction in Social Studies Grades 4–5–6: Negroes in American Life* (Chicago: Chicago Bureau of Curriculum, 1942), 25.

19. Woodson, *Negro Makers of History,* 5.

20. Johnson, Herdeg, and Lusson, *Supplementary Units, Grades 4–5–6,* 26.

21. Melville Herskovits, *The Myth of the Negro Past* (Boston: Beacon Press, 1941), 32.

22. Johnson, Herdeg, and Lusson, *Supplementary Units, Grades 4–5–6,* 28.

23. Johnson, Herdeg, and Lusson, *Supplementary Units, Grades 4–5–6,* 34–35.

24. Johnson, Herdeg, and Lusson, *Supplementary Units, Grades 4–5–6,* 25.

25. Johnson, Herdeg, and Lusson, *Supplementary Units, Grades 4–5–6,* 25, 26.

26. Von Eschen, *Race Against Empire,* 13.

27. Johnson, Herdeg, and Lusson, *Supplementary Units, Grades 1–2–3,* 12–13.

28. Au, Brown, and Calderon, *Reclaiming the Multicultural Roots of U.S. Curriculum,* 123.

29. Johnson, Herdeg, and Lusson, *Supplementary Units, Grades 4–5–6,* 16.

30. Johnson, Herdeg, and Lusson, *Supplementary Units, Grades 4–5–6,* 16.

31. Benjamin Brawley, *A Short History of the American Negro,* rev. ed. (New York, Macmillan, 1919), 10.

32. Woodson, *Negro Makers of History,* 16.

33. Merl Eppse, *The Negro, Too, in American History* (Nashville: National Educational Publishing, 1943): 43.

34. J. A. Rogers, "The Negro Explorer," *Crisis*, January 1940, 7.

35. Johnson, Herdeg and Lusson, *Supplementary Units, Grades 4–5–6*, 16.

36. Johnson, Herdeg and Lusson, *Supplementary Units, Grades 4–5–6*, 16, 18–19.

37. Johnson, Herdeg and Lusson, *Supplementary Units, Grades 4–5–6*, 20.

38. Rogers, "The Negro Explorer," 7.

39. Chara Haeussler Bohan, Lauren Yarnell Bradshaw, and Wade Hampton Morris Jr., "The Mint Julep Consensus: An Analysis of Late 19th Century Southern and Northern Textbooks and Their Impact on the History Curriculum," *Journal of Social Studies Research* 44 (2020): 140.

40. For more on the battles over textbook content, see Jonathan Zimmerman, *Whose America? Culture Wars in the Public Schools* (Cambridge, MA: Harvard University Press, 2002), 34.

41. W. E. B. Du Bois, *Black Reconstruction in America 1860-1880*, originally published 1935 (New York: Free Press, 1998), 713.

42. Lawrence Reddick, "Racial Attitudes in American History Textbooks of the South," *Journal of Negro History* 19, no. 3 (1934): 234.

43. William Johnson, Leo Herdeg, and Mary Lusson, *Supplementary Units for the Course of Instruction in Social Studies, Grades 7–8* (Chicago: Chicago Bureau of Curriculum, 1942), I.

44. Johnson, Herdeg and Lusson, *Supplementary Units, Grades 7–8*, 2.

45. Leah Washburn, "Accounts of Slavery: An Analysis of United States History Textbooks from 1900 to 1992," *Theory and Research in Social Education* 25, no. 4 (1997): 470–91.

46. Mabel B. Casner and Ralph Henry Gabriel, *Exploring American History* (New York: Harcourt, Brace, 1931), 398.

47. Beeby, *America's Roots in the Past*, 309–10.

48. Beeby, *America's Roots in the Past*, 310–11.

49. Johnson, Herdeg, and Lusson, *Supplementary Units, Grades 7–8*, 10.

50. Johnson, Herdeg, and Lusson, *Supplementary Units, Grades 7–8*, 11–12.

51. Johnson, Herdeg, and Lusson, *Supplementary Units, Grades 4–5–6*, 10.

52. Johnson, Herdeg, and Lusson, *Supplementary Units, Grades 7–8*, 12.

53. Johnson, Herdeg, and Lusson, *Supplementary Units, Grades 7–8*, 12.

54. Johnson, Herdeg, and Lusson, *Supplementary Units, Grades 7–8*, 12.

55. Casner and Gabriel, *Exploring American History*, 442.

56. Washburn, "Accounts of Slavery," 479.

57. Johnson, Herdeg, and Lusson, *Supplementary Units, Grades 7–8*, 12.

58. Johnson, Herdeg, and Lusson, *Supplementary Units, Grades 7–8*, 16.

59. Reddick, "Racial Attitudes in American History Textbooks," 245–46.

60. Johnson, Herdeg, and Lusson, *Supplementary Units, Grades 7–8*, 16.

61. Johnson, Herdeg, and Lusson, *Supplementary Units, Grades 7–8*, 16.

62. Johnson, Herdeg, and Lusson, *Supplementary Units, Grades 7–8*, 16–17.

63. Johnson, Herdeg, and Lusson, *Supplementary Units, Grades 7–8*, 37.

64. Casner and Gabriel, *Exploring American History*, 503.

65. West and West, *The Story of Our Country*, 383.

66. Casner and Gabriel, *Exploring American History*, 503.

67. Casner and Gabriel, *Exploring American History*, 503.

68. West and West, *The Story of Our Country*, 383.

69. Johnson, Herdeg, and Lusson, *Supplementary Units, Grades 7–8*, 17.

70. Johnson, Herdeg, and Lusson, *Supplementary Units, Grades 7–8*, 17–18.

71. Woodson, *Negro Makers of History*, 295.

72. Brown, "Counter-Memory and Race," 58.

73. Johnson, Herdeg, and Lusson, *Supplementary Units, Grades 1–2–3*, 2.

74. Johnson, Herdeg, and Lusson, *Supplementary Units, Grades 7–8*, 55.

75. Johnson, Herdeg, and Lusson, *Supplementary Units, Grades 1–2–3*, 5.

76. Johnson, Herdeg, and Lusson, *Supplementary Units, Grades 7–8*, 63.

77. Anthony L. Brown, Ryan M. Crawley, and LaGarrett J. King, "Black Civitas: An Examination of Carter Woodson's Contributions to Teaching About Race, Citizenship, and the Black Soldier," *Theory and Research in Social Education* 39, no. 2 (2011): 278.

78. Johnson, Herdeg, and Lusson, *Supplementary Units, Grades 7–8*, 40.

79. Johnson, Herdeg, and Lusson, *Supplementary Units, Grades 7–8*, 43.

80. Carter G. Woodson, *The Negro in Our History* (Washington, DC: Associated Publishers, 1922), 328.

81. Pero Gaglo Dagbovie, *What Is African American History?* (Cambridge: Polity Press, 2015), 7.

82. Brawley, *A Short History of the American Negro*, 81.

83. Woodson, *The Negro in Our History*, 339–40.

84. Zimmerman, *Whose America?*, 10.

85. Madeline Morgan, "Chicago Schools Teach Negro History," *Elementary English Review* 21, no. 3 (1944): 109.

86. LaGarrett King, "When Lions Write History: Black History Textbooks, African American Educators, and the Alternative Black Curriculum in Social Studies Education, 1890–1940," *Multicultural Education* 22, no. 1 (2014): 2.

Poem

1. "Poem for Madeline Morgan," MSM Papers, box 9, folder 46.

Chapter 4: "And Quite the Pride of the Middle West"

1. Namuh Brascher, "Honor School Chief for New History Course Plan," *Chicago Defender*, June 20, 1942.

2. "Chicago Public Schools, Dinner for Supt. Johnson," MSM Papers, box 7, folder 1.

3. Brascher, "Honor School Chief for New History Course Plan."

4. Association for the Study of Negro Life and History, "Proceedings of the Twenty-Eighth Annual Meeting of the Association for the Study of Negro Life

and History, Held at Detroit, Michigan, October 29–31, 1943," *Journal of Negro History* 29, no. 1 (1944): 2.

5. Association for the Study of Negro Life and History, "Proceedings of the Twenty-Eighth Annual Meeting of the Association for the Study of Negro Life and History," 3.

6. Gertrude Robinson to Madeline Morgan, December 3, 1943, MSM Papers, box 9, folder 46.

7. "The Spingarn Medal," *Crisis*, June 1914, 88.

8. Gertrude Robinson to Madeline Morgan, December 3, 1943, MSM Papers, box 9, folder 46.

9. "A Fundamental Attack on Prejudice," *Pittsburgh Courier*, June 26, 1943.

10. Judge William H. Hastie, "Why I Resigned!," *Chicago Defender*, February 6, 1943.

11. Tamara Beauboeuf-Lafontant, "The New Howard Woman: Lucy Diggs Slowe and the Education of a Modern Black Femininity," *Meridians: Feminism, Race, Transnationalism* 17, no. 1 (2018): 42. For more on Lucy Diggs Slowe, see Carroll L. L. Miller and Anne S. Pruitt Logan, *Faithful to the Task at Hand: The Life of Lucy Diggs Slowe* (New York: SUNY Press, 2012); Linda M. Perkins, "Lucy Diggs Slowe: Champion of the Self-Determination of African-American Women in Higher Education," *Journal of Negro History* 81, no. 4 (1996): 89–104.

12. "Sorority Honors Chicagoans," *Chicago Defender*, March 4, 1944.

13. "Race Relations Honor Roll: Nation-Wide Poll Selects 12 Negroes and 6 Whites Who Made 'Worthy Contributions to Boost Inter-Racial Unity' During 1943," *New York Amsterdam News*, February 19, 1944.

14. A. M. Wendell Malliett, "'City Wide Integration of Negro History' Program Challenges Authorities to Improve Race-Relations," *New York Amsterdam News*, March 18, 1944.

15. Russell W. Smith to Madeline Morgan, October 11, 1943, MSM Papers, box 2, folder 20.

16. Houston R. Jackson to Madeline Morgan, November 24, 1943, MSM Papers, box 2, folder 20.

17. "Seek Negro History Classes in East Liverpool School System," *Cleveland Call and Post*, May 27, 1944.

18. Walter E. Morial to Madeline Morgan, June 24, 1943, MSM Papers, box 2, folder 20.

19. Cohen T. Simpson to Madeline Morgan, February 10, 1944, MSM Papers, box 2, folder 20.

20. Pero G. Dagbovie, *The Early Black History Movement, Carter G. Woodson, and Lorenzo Johnston Greene* (Urbana: University of Illinois Press, 2007), 99.

21. "Chicago Goes Forward with Madeline Morgan," *Negro History Bulletin* 6, no. 5 (1943): 112.

22. "Chicago Goes Forward with Madeline Morgan."

23. E. Franklin Frazier, *Black Bourgeoisie* (Glencoe, IL: Free Press, 1957), 94.

24. Marybeth Gasman, "Sisters in Service: African American Sororities and Philanthropic Support of Education," in *Women and Philanthropy in Education*, ed. Andrea Walton (Bloomington: Indiana University Press, 2005), 197.

25. Paula Giddings, *Searching for Sisterhood: Delta Sigma Theta and the Challenge of the Black Sorority Movement* (New York: Morrow, 1988), 88.

26. Giddings, *Searching for Sisterhood*, 112.

27. C. G. Woodson, "Negro Historians of Our Times," *Negro History Bulletin* 8, no. 7 (1945): 155.

28. Woodson, "Negro Historians of Our Times," 159.

29. Pero Gaglo Dagbovie, "Black Women Historians from the Late 19th Century to the Dawning of the Civil Rights Movement," *Journal of African American History* 89, no. 3 (2004): 241–61.

30. "Questions on the February Issue," *Negro History Bulletin* 6, no. 6 (1943): 133.

31. "Editorial Comment: Why a Journal of Negro Education?" *Journal of Negro Education* 1, no. 1 (1932): 3.

32. Martin D. Jenkins to Madeline Morgan, November 28, 1942, MSM Papers, box 6, folder 19.

33. Madeline R. Morgan, "Chicago School Curriculum Includes Negro Achievements," *Journal of Negro Education* 13, no. 1 (1944): 120–23.

34. Lester B. Granger, "Phylon Profile II: Willard S. Townsend," *Phylon* 5, no. 4 (1944): 331.

35. Willard S. Townsend to Madeline Morgan, September 11, 1943, MSM Papers, box 2, folder 20.

36. "Mayor Kelly's Race Commission," *Chicago Defender*, August 7, 1943.

37. "23 Dead, 650 Hurt as Violence Grows: Wave of Outbreaks Spreads over Nation," *Chicago Defender*, June 26, 1943.

38. "Roosevelt Urged to Uproot the Causes of Recent Race Riots," *Christian Science Monitor*, June 29, 1943.

39. "Roosevelt Urged to Uproot the Causes of Recent Race Riots."

40. "Brown Studies," *Time*, June 21, 1943, 48.

41. Paul Milkman, *PM: A New Deal in Journalism: 1940–1948* (Denver: Outskirts Press, 2016). *PM*, which ran from 1940 to 1948, was the work of publisher Robert Ingersoll, who had overseen the rebirth of *Time* and *Fortune* and helped launch the magazine *Life* before starting his own publication. From its inception *PM* staked out liberal/leftist positions on a range of issues including its support for militant antifascism, an endorsement of labor organizing and trade unionism, and an unflinching opposition to antisemitism and anti-Black racism.

42. Fletcher Wilson, "How Chicago Teaches Whites to Respect Negroes and Negroes to Respect Themselves," *PM*, September 5, 1943, 14.

43. Wilson, "How Chicago Teaches Whites to Respect Negroes and Negroes to Respect Themselves," 15.

44. Evelyn B. Higginbotham, *Righteous Discontent: The Women's Movement in the Black Baptist Church, 1880–1920* (Cambridge, MA: Harvard University Press, 1993), 186.

45. Higginbotham, *Righteous Discontent*, 187.

46. Madeline R. Morgan, "Chicago Schools Teach Negro History," *Elementary English Review* 21, no. 3 (1944): 109.

47. Morgan, "Chicago Schools Teach Negro History," 108.

48. Laura J. Ladance to Madeline Morgan, September 20, 1943, MSM Papers, box 2, folder 20.

49. "Newark Youth Slain in Schoolboy Brawls That Bring Ten Riot Calls to the Police," *New York Times*, June 5, 1943.

50. "23 Dead, 650 Hurt as Violence Grows."

51. Ladance to Morgan, September 20, 1943.

52. Edward J. Escobar, *Race, Police, and the Making of a Political Identity: Mexican Americans and the Los Angeles Police Department, 1900–1945* (Berkeley: University of California Press, 1999), 236.

53. Robert Hill Lane to Madeline Morgan, November 29, 1943, MSM Papers, box 2, folder 20.

54. National Urban League, *Racial Conflict, a Home Front Danger: Lessons of the Detroit Riots* (New York: National Urban League, 1943), 3.

55. National Urban League, *Racial Conflict*, 7.

56. "Demand FDR Act in Riots: Detroit Death Toll Reaches 15 in Clashes: Martial Law Declared by Governor as City Cops Fail," *Chicago Defender*, June 26, 1943.

57. "Army Rules Detroit; 23 Die: Homes Fired, Shops Looted in Race Riots," *Chicago Defender*, June 22, 1943.

58. "Detroit Public Schools, Interracial Policy, 1945," MSM Papers, box 9, folder 1.

59. Anne-Lise Halvorsen and Jeffrey Mirel, "Intercultural Education in Detroit, 1943–1954," *Paedagogica Historica* 49, no. 3 (2013).

60. "Detroit Public Schools, Interracial Policy, 1945."

61. Marion Edwan to Madeline Morgan, February 8, 1944, MSM Papers, box 2, folder 20.

62. Morgan, "Chicago Schools Teach Negro History," 108.

63. Morton Brooks, "Correspondence, Morton Brooks (Italy), 1943," MSM Papers, box 2, folder 15.

64. Brooks, "Correspondence, Morton Brooks (Italy), 1943."

Chapter 5: "Erase the Color Line from the Blackboards of America"

1. Grace Markwell, "Untitled Student Responses," MSM Papers, box 6, folder 26, 4.

2. Grace Markwell, "Interracial Possibilities," MSM Papers, box 6, folder 26, 4.

3. Madeline Morgan, "The Study of Negro History," MSM Papers, box 4, folder 33, 1.

4. Wayne Au, Anthony L. Brown, and Dolores Calderon, *Reclaiming the Multicultural Roots of U.S. Curriculum* (New York: Teachers College Press, 2016), 124.

5. Morgan, "Study of Negro History," 1.

6. Madeline Morgan, "'Chicago Public Schools Project, 1942' (ASNLH 1975)," MSM Papers, box 2, folder 12, 1.

7. Carter G. Woodson, "Negro History Week," *Journal of Negro History* 11, no. 2 (1926): 240.

8. Madeline Morgan, "Chicago Schools Teach Negro History," *Elementary English Review* 21, no. 3 (March 1944): 109.

9. Madeline Morgan, "Chicago School Curriculum Includes Negro Achievements," *Journal of Negro Education* 13, no. 1 (Winter 1944): 123.

10. "Untitled Student Response," MSM Papers, box 7, folder 27.

11. James Anderson, "Secondary School History Textbooks and the Treatment of Black History," in *The State of Afro-American History, Past, Present, and Future*, ed. Darlene Clarke Hine (Baton Rouge: Louisiana State University Press, 1986).

12. William Johnson, Leo Herdeg, and Mary Lusson, *Supplementary Units for the Course of Instruction in Social Studies Grades 4–5–6: Negroes in American Life* (Chicago: Chicago Bureau of Curriculum, 1942), 26.

13. "Untitled Student Response," MSM Papers, box 7, folder 27.

14. "Untitled Student Response," MSM Papers, box 7, folder 27.

15. "Untitled Student Response," MSM Papers, box 7, folder 27.

16. "Thousands View Bud Biliken Americanism Day Parade and Picnic," *Chicago Defender*, August 17, 1940.

17. "Untitled Student Response," MSM Papers, box 7, folder 27.

18. "Untitled Student Response," MSM Papers, box 7, folder 27.

19. "Untitled Student Response," MSM Papers, box 7, folder 27.

20. J. Burns to Madeline Morgan, October 4, 1944, MSM Papers [manuscript], 1941–1945, United States, World War II Miscellaneous Collection, Chicago History Museum (hereafter WWII Misc.).

21. L. B. Winston to Madeline Morgan, June 6, 1944, MSM Papers [manuscript], WWII Misc.

22. George M. Cooper to Madeline Morgan, March 12, 1945, MSM Papers [manuscript], WWII Misc.

23. Edward Butler to Madeline Morgan, November 5, 1943, MSM Papers [manuscript], WWII Misc.

24. "Untitled Student Response," MSM Papers, box 7, folder 27.

25. Anthony L. Brown, Ryan M. Crowley, and LaGarrett J. King, "Black Civitas: An Examination of Carter G. Woodson's Contributions to Teaching About Race, Citizenship, and the Black Soldier," *Theory and Research in Social Education* 39, no. 2 (2011): 280.

26. "Untitled Student Response," MSM Papers, box 7, folder 27.

27. "Untitled Student Response," MSM Papers, box 7, folder 27.

28. "Untitled Student Response," MSM Papers, box 7, folder 27.

29. "Untitled Student Response," MSM Papers, box 7, folder 27.

30. Morgan, "Chicago Schools Teach Negro History," 107.

31. National Council for the Social Studies, *The Social Studies Mobilize for Victory: A Statement of Wartime Policy Adopted by the National Council for the Social Studies* (Washington, DC: National Council for the Social Studies, 1942), 5, 16.

32. National Council for the Social Studies, *The Social Studies Mobilize for Victory*, 8, 10–11.

33. National Council for the Social Studies, *The Social Studies Mobilize for Victory*, 11–12.

34. Chase W. Linwood, *Wartime Social Studies in the Elementary Classroom* (Washington, DC: National Council for the Social Studies, 1943), 31.

35. Markwell, "Interracial Possibilities," 1.

36. Zoe Burkholder, "From 'Wops and Dagoes and Hunkies' to 'Caucasian': Changing Racial Discourse in American Classrooms During World War II," *History of Education Quarterly* 50, no. 3 (2010): 339.

37. Markwell, "Interracial Possibilities," 1.

38. Morgan, "Chicago Schools Teach Negro History," 108.

39. Markwell, "Interracial Possibilities," 2.

40. Markwell, "Interracial Possibilities," 6.

41. Markwell, "Interracial Possibilities," 7.

42. Helen Laville, "'If the Time Is Not Ripe, Then It Is Your Job to Ripen the Time!': The Transformation of the YWCA in the USA from Segregated Association to Interracial Organization, 1930–1965," *Women's History Review* 15, no. 3 (July 2006): 359–83.

43. Grace Markwell, "The Supplementary Units in the White School," MSM Papers, box 5, folder 20, 1.

44. Markwell, "The Supplementary Units in the White School," 2.

45. Markwell, "Interracial Possibilities," 3.

46. Unnamed student to Madeline Morgan, January 14, 1944, MSM Papers, box 6, folder 26.

47. Grace Markwell, "Student Reactions to Morgan Visit," MSM Papers, box 6, folder 26, 1–4.

48. For a history of Black domestic work, see Rebecca Sharpless, *Cooking in Other Women's Kitchens: Domestic Workers in the South, 1865–1960* (Chapel Hill: University of North Carolina Press, 2010).

49. Markwell, "Student Reactions to Morgan Visit," 1.

50. Markwell, "Student Reactions to Morgan Visit," 4.

51. Markwell, "Student Reactions to Morgan Visit," 5.

52. Jonna Perrillo, *Uncivil Rights: Teachers, Unions, and the Battle for School Equity* (Chicago: University of Chicago Press, 2012), 61.

53. Markwell, "Student Reactions to Morgan Visit," 4.

54. Grace Markwell to Ralston Gray, April 14, 1944, MSM Papers, box 6, folder 26.

55. "Review Work of Social Service Group at Gross," *Suburban Magnet* (Brookfield, IL), June 1, 1944.

56. Markwell, "The Supplementary Units in the White School," 3.

57. Illinois Council for the Social Studies, "Interracial Cooperation," MSM Papers, box 9, folder 14, 7.

58. Grace Markwell, "White Teacher Wants Personality Sketches," *Chicago Defender*, August 5, 1944.

59. Markwell, "The Supplementary Units in the White School," 3.

Chapter Six: "This Crucial War for Democracy"

1. Mayor's Commission on Human Relations, *Race Relations in Chicago: Report of the Mayor's Commission on Human Relations for 1945* (Chicago: City of Chicago, 1945), 15.

2. "Goebbels in the Classroom," *Chicago Defender*, October 6, 1945.

3. Cherry McGee Banks, *Improving Multicultural Education: Lessons from the Intergroup Education Movement* (New York: Teachers College Press, 2004), 131.

4. St. Clair Drake and Horace R. Cayton, *The Black Metropolis: A Study of Negro Life in a Northern City* (Chicago: University of Chicago Press, 1945), 8.

5. Mayor's Committee on Race Relations, *Race Relations in Chicago: Report of the Mayor's Committee on Race Relations* (Chicago: City of Chicago, 1944), 13.

6. For more on these fires and their human toll, see Joe Allen, *People Wasn't Meant to Burn: A True Story of Race, Murder, and Justice in Chicago* (Chicago: Haymarket Books, 2011).

7. Arnold R. Hirsch, *Making the Second Ghetto: Race and Housing Policy in Chicago, 1940–1960* (New York: Cambridge University Press, 1983), 40.

8. Mayor's Committee on Race Relations, *Race Relations in Chicago*, 15.

9. "The No-Transfer Order," *Chicago Defender*, October 28, 1944.

10. "Educator Is Injured as House Is Bombed," *New York Times*, September 22, 1944.

11. Roger Biles, "Edward J. Kelly: New Deal Machine Builder," in *The Mayors: The Chicago Political Tradition*, ed. Paul M. Green and Melvin G. Holli (Carbondale: Southern Illinois University Press, 2005), 124. Biles explains that although Kelly's political downfall, like that of Johnson, is often couched as an issue of his political corruption, this malfeasance and graft was endemic to and accepted by the Chicago Democratic machine and by its voters as well. On the other hand, Kelly's stance on Black access to housing in the postwar period met with massive resistance and ultimately cost him his mayoralty as "one new issue that arose in the mid-forties crystallized public opinion against Kelly: the open housing controversy. Jealously guarding their 'turf', South Side whites braced to resist racial 'blockbusting' and sneeringly referred to neighborhood swimming pools which blacks seemed to monopolize as 'Kelly's inkwells.' The mayor's repeated pledge to guarantee the availability of housing city wide to blacks galvanized the public. . . . The Germans, Irish, and Poles shared one thing in common—an opposition to Kelly's stand on open housing."

12. Mayor's Commission on Human Relations, *Race Relations in Chicago: Report of the Mayor's Commission on Human Relations for 1946* (Chicago: City of Chicago, 1946), 72.

13. Timothy B. Neary, *Crossing Parish Boundaries: Race, Sports, and Catholic Youth in Chicago, 1914–1954* (Chicago: University of Chicago Press, 2016), 161, 173.

14. Neary, *Crossing Parish Boundaries*, 176.

15. Samuel Stratton, "Democracy Only Possible Through Brotherhood," MSM Papers, box 13, folder 6, 4.

16. Stratton, "Democracy Only Possible Through Brotherhood."

17. George W. Bowles to Madeline Morgan, MSM Papers, box 2, folder 20.

18. Bess Periman to Madeline Morgan, MSM Papers, box 2, folder 20.

19. Drusilla McCormick to Madeline Morgan, MSM Papers, box 2, folder 20.

20. Mary McLeod Bethune to Madeline Morgan, February 6, 1947, MSM Papers, box 9, folder 38.

21. Bethune to Morgan, February 6, 1947.

22. Mayor's Committee on Race Relations, *Race Relations in Chicago* (1944), 16.

23. Banks, *Improving Multicultural Education*, 131.

24. "Illinois General Assembly, House Bill No. 251, 1945–1946," MSM Papers, box 9, folder 15.

25. "Ill. House Okays Negro History in Public Schools," *Chicago Defender*, May 26, 1945.

26. "Illinois General Assembly, House Bill No. 251, 1945–1946," MSM Papers, box 9, folder 15.

27. "Editorial: Suggestions to the New School Board," *Pittsburgh Courier*, October 5, 1946.

28. Herold C. Hunt, "Chicago's Intercultural Relations Program," *Chicago Schools Journal: An Educational Magazine for Chicago Teachers* 31, nos. 3–4 (1949): 113.

29. Hunt, "Chicago's Intercultural Relations Program," 115.

30. Michael Daryl Scott, "Postwar Pluralism, *Brown v. Board of Education*, and the Origins of Multicultural Education," *Journal of American History* 91, no. 1 (2004): 72.

Epilogue

1. Madeline Robinson Stratton, *Negroes Who Helped Build America* (Boston: Ginn and Company, 1965); Madeline R. Stratton, *Strides Forward: Afro-American Biographies* (Lexington, MA: Ginn and Company, 1973).

2. Ian Rocksborough Smith, *Black Public History in Chicago: Civil Rights Activism from World War II until the Cold War* (Champaign: University of Illinois Press, 2018), 35.

3. Dyan Watson, Jess Hagopian, and Wayne Au, *Teaching for Black Lives* (Milwaukee: Rethinking Schools, 2018), 1–2.

4. Erik Gleibermann, "New College Board Curriculum Puts the African Diaspora in the Spotlight," *Washington Post*, September 8, 2020.

5. Madina Touré, "Black Studies Curriculum Begins to Take Shape for New York City Public Schools," *Politico*, September 28, 2021, https://www.politico.com/states/new-york/city-hall/story/2021/09/28/black-studies-curriculum-begins-to-take-shape-for-new-york-city-public-schools-1391471.

6. Nikita Stewart, "'We Are Committing Educational 'Malpractice': Why Slavery Is Mistaught—and Worse—in American Schools," *New York Times*, August 19, 2019.

7. "Illinois General Assembly, House Bill No. 251, 1945–1946," MSM Papers, box 9, folder 15.

8. Board of Education, City of Chicago, *The Chicago Public Schools in Wartime: Published as the Annual Report of the Superintendent of Schools for the School Years 1941–1942, 1942–1943* (Chicago: Board of Education, 1943), 186.

9. Janice K. Jackson, "The 1619 Project and Chicago Public Schools," September 17, 2019, https://blog.cps.edu/2019/09/17/the-1619-project-and-chicago-public-schools.

INDEX

abolition, 64–71

abolitionists, 69–70

Administrative Committee on Intercultural and Interracial Education (Detroit), 106, 107

Advanced Placement (AP) program, 155

Africa, 54–61; as advanced society, 59–60; Black American connection to, 54–55, 58–59; character and capacity of people of, 60–61; distorted picture of, 54; and early Black history movement, 55, 171n10; marginalization of, 56–57; myth of dark continent of, 57; objective research and scientific observation about, 57; old kingdoms of, 59–60; providing information about history and culture of, 57–59; reconceptualization of, xix, 55–57; in white-authored textbooks, 56

African Diaspora Consortium, 155

African Heroes and Heroines (Woodson), xiii, 55

Afrocentric education, 115

agency, Black, 52, 61, 70

Airport Housing Project, 143

Alabama State Teachers' Association, 91

Allen, Doris, 131

Alpha Kappa Alpha, 88, 93

alternative Black curriculum: Black identity in, 79; choice of source materials for, 53; early Black history movement and, xii–xiv; organizations in Chicago shaping, 25; redefining Africa in, 55, 57; reframing world and US history in, 52; *Supplementary Units* as, xix, 51–80

American Association of School Administrators, 107

American exceptionalism, 46, 78

"Americanism," 78

American Negro Exposition (1940), xviii, 27–31, 32–33, 51, 138n3

Americans All, Immigrants All (radio program), 37–38

America's Roots in the Past (Beeby), 10, 56, 66

Anderson, Clara, 45

Anderson, Marian, 52, 86, 128, 134, 145

Anderson, Patricia, 130

Anti-Negro Propaganda in Textbooks (NAACP), 40

anti-prejudice education, 36–37

antisemitism, xiv

A. O. Sexton Elementary School (Chicago), 153

AP (Advanced Placement) program, 155